How to create

A Small Garden Sanctuary

Transform Small Gardens with

Water, Petals & Wild Ideas

No Experience Needed

R C Brook

TABLE OF CONTENTS

CHAPTER ONE

INTRODUCTION

Welcome to your garden sanctuary

(kettle on, secateurs ready)

Acouple of years ago, I moved into a modest townhouse with a tiny outdoor space. It wasn't exactly a dream garden. No lawn, no flower beds, no romantic trailing roses or chirping fountains. Just some tired-looking concrete slabs, a few confused weeds, and a hedge that appeared to have aspirations of world domination. It wasn't a garden; it was a forgotten corner. A slightly dishevelled, slightly sulky space.

But I had a vision. I pictured a sanctuary, a peaceful little retreat that would feel like my own personal Eden. Somewhere I could sip with colour and life, a celebration of texture and fragrance, of greenery and calm. I wasn't after a grand estate. I just wanted a garden that would feel like a warm hug.

That very spot, once dull and concrete-clad, is now a small but mighty oasis. There are flowers that bloom on cue, herbs that catch the sun, and a little bench that's seen its fair share of coffee mornings, deep thoughts, and half-eaten biscuits (some stolen by curious pigeons). It's not perfect, and it's still evolving, but it's mine. And that transformation, watching something unloved become something cherished, was nothing short of magic.

This book is born from that experience. It's for anyone who's ever looked at a dull, overlooked patch of ground and thought, "Could I make this something special?" The answer is yes. And it doesn't matter if you're working with a balcony, a courtyard, or a postage-stamp patio; beauty and peace don't require acreage. They just require intention, a touch of creativity, and a willingness to get your hands dirty.

Gardening, for me, isn't just about the end result, it's about the process. The mindfulness of planting. The hope of watching things grow. The joy of discovering that even when life feels chaotic, a few minutes tending to a pot of lavender can ground you in a way few things can. There's a rhythm to it. A kind of peaceful pulse that connects us to nature, to the seasons, and to something wonderfully primal.

My love for gardening started young. My grandfather was a gardener in every sense of the word, not by profession, but by heart. I remember trailing after him, tiny trowel in hand, helping (and occasionally hindering) as he planted and pruned. He taught me patience, observation, and the quiet satisfaction of coaxing life from soil. I still remember the first time I planted a seed and watched it grow. It felt like alchemy. Pure, green magic.

As life became busier and noisier, I found myself craving that kind of simplicity again. A retreat from the notifications, the deadlines, the endless to-do lists. And so I returned to the garden, not just to grow plants, but to grow calm. That tiny space became my sanctuary. A place to think, to be still, to reconnect.

This book is for anyone, beginner or experienced, who wants to do the same. It's a guide, yes, but also an invitation. You don't need to know Latin plant names (although we'll drop a few in to sound fancy), and you certainly don't need to be a horticulturist. You just need a little patch, a bit of curiosity, and a desire to create something beautiful.

I'll walk you through the whole process, from designing your space and choosing tools, to selecting plants and tackling pests (without going full pesticide warrior). You'll learn how to work with the seasons, choose plants that bring joy all year round, and keep everything thriving without having to give up your weekends or remortgage your house.

What sets this book apart is its focus on adaptability and simplicity. Gardens aren't one-size-fits-all. They vary depending on location, climate, and personality. Whether you're in a bustling city or a sleepy village, there's a garden waiting to grow into your life. And it doesn't have to cost a fortune. You'll find tips for creating beauty on a budget, repurposing everyday items, and making the most of what you already have.

I'll also share stories, because gardens are full of them. Moments of triumph (like the first tomato that didn't look like a shrivelled raisin) and moments of learning (like realising that 'full sun' really means full sun, not "a bit of dappled light between 2:10 and 2:15pm").

And don't worry, this isn't going to be dry and textbook-y. Think of me as a slightly muddy, tea-loving friend, here to cheer you on, laugh with you at the mistakes, and celebrate the successes (including the ones that involve finally outsmarting a slug).

Before we dig in, a quick word for my lovely friends on both sides of the Atlantic (my mother is English and my father is American so I'm a TransAtlantic, I think...) you'll notice I use both UK and US gardening terms throughout this book. 'Green fingers' and 'green thumbs' are equally welcome here. Whether you're calling it a 'garden' or a 'yard', planting in a 'pot' or a 'container', it's all about creating a space that nurtures you as much as the plants within it. But I may forget some!

So whether you're brand new to gardening or just looking to reimagine a small space, I hope this book helps you create a haven of your own. A space that reflects your style, nurtures your wellbeing, and brings a little joy into your every day.

Let's dig in now, shall we?

CHAPTER TWO

SPACE

Designing the garden *of your dreams,*
even if it's the size of a biscuit tin

Right, my green-fingered friend, let's start at the very beginning (it's a very good place to start, as Julie Andrews once wisely sang). Before we dive headfirst into bags of compost, bewildering plant labels, and all things muddy, let's pause. Take a deep breath, look at your little plot (or balcony, or patio, no judgement here), and say to yourself: "This is my sanctuary-to-be, even if currently it looks more like a storage space for unloved furniture." Ready? Excellent, let's get designing!

Different Styles

Gardens, like people, have personalities. You might be drawn to something tidy and minimal, or perhaps you love wild abandon. Here are a few to get your creative juices flowing:

• **Zen/Minimalist**: Clean lines, gravel paths, bamboo, simple evergreens, and water features. Think calm. Think serenity. Perfect for small spaces that need a touch of balance.

• **Cottage Garden**: Overflowing with colour and blooms, winding paths, and whimsical charm. Hollyhocks and foxgloves waving like polite neighbours. A little chaotic. Very cheerful.

• **Modern Urban**: Sleek containers, bold architectural plants, privacy screens, and smart lighting. Ideal for balconies, rooftops, and patios in the heart of a buzzing city.

• **Wildlife Haven**: Pollinator-friendly, native plants, log piles, bird baths, and insect hotels. A garden that's alive with bees, butterflies, and birdsong. Low-maintenance and rich in biodiversity.

Don't be afraid to mix and match. Maybe your soul says "Zen" but your heart says "sunflowers." Go with what makes you smile. The style is your story, this space is an expression of who you are.

Focal Points and Features

Every good design has a focal point, or a few. These are the eye-catchers, the elements that ground your garden and give it structure.

• **Seating**: A bistro table, a swing chair, or a simple bench beneath your favourite tree. Your throne. Your thinking spot. Your tea station. Consider adding outdoor cushions, throws, or even a small side table for your mug of tea or book. A swing seat or hammock can add a gentle sense of movement. If space allows, try positioning your seating where it catches the morning sun or where you can admire your favourite plantings.

• **Water Feature**: From a bubbling urn to a small pond with floating lily pads. Nothing says tranquillity like the gentle sound of trickling water. Even a small solar-powered fountain in a bowl can transform the mood of your space. A birdbath doubles as a focal point and a wildlife haven. If you're feeling adventurous, a tiny pond in an old sink or barrel can attract frogs and add a lush feel.

• **Sculpture or Ornament**: A quirky gnome? A sleek steel sphere? A bird bath with character? One well-placed object can set the tone. Think beyond the garden centre catalogue. A found object, like a driftwood sculpture or a salvaged window frame, can add personality and spark conversation. Tuck your ornament into planting so it feels discovered rather than plonked.

• **Statement Plant**: A tree fern, an acer, or a particularly fabulous hydrangea. Let something steal the spotlight. Use an oversized pot to lift it up, or plant it where it naturally draws the eye, like at the end of a path or beside your seating. Ornamental grasses, architectural succulents, or even a topiary in an unusual shape can turn heads and create cohesion.

These elements give the garden form and purpose, even when the plants are resting. Even the smallest balcony can have a feature, sometimes it's just the view you've chosen to frame.

Understanding Your Climate

Know your zone. Are you coastal with salty winds? Urban with heat pockets? Shady or sunny? This will guide your plant choices and layout. Be realistic and work with your environment, not against it.• **Sun Maps**: Spend a day noting where the sun lands at different times. What's in full sun at 10am might be shady by 2pm. Tracking this across the seasons helps you position plants where they'll thrive not just survive.

• **Shelter**: Can you use existing fences or walls for protection? Consider wind direction and exposure. A row of pots can act as a windbreak; climbers on trellises can create microclimates.

• **Soil**: Is it sandy, clay, loam? Acidic or alkaline? Even if you're container gardening, this matters. A quick soil test can save you heaps of heartache and money.

If you're in the **UK**, remember the north tends to be cooler and wetter, while the south is milder and drier. Scottish gardens often face shorter growing seasons, while southern English plots can bake in summer. On top of that, coastal areas may battle wind and salt, while inland cities often experience warmer microclimates.

In the **US**, gardeners rely on USDA hardiness zones. Zone 3 (hello, Minnesota) has a vastly different calendar than Zone 9 (looking at you, Florida). In the northern states, the growing season can be brief but intense. In the south, the season may be longer but requires heat-tolerant plants and strategies to conserve water.

Adaptation is key. Choose plants that love your environment instead of battling it. Check plant labels or do a quick online lookup to match the right plant to your place. You'll save yourself a world of wilting, sighing, and emergency shade-rigging.

Budgeting

Gardens can be created on a shoestring or with a bit more wiggle room. Here's how to make the most of your money:

Start small: Focus on one area and build from there. A single border or a herb planter is a perfect beginning.

Reuse and repurpose: Pallets become planters; tins become herb pots. Old sinks make great wildlife ponds. A tired chair becomes a flower throne.

Cuttings and swaps: Share plants with friends or neighbours. Join local groups or online forums. Gardeners are wonderfully generous.

Sales and seconds: Garden centres often have clearance sections for plants that look a bit scruffy but just need love.

Remember, time is a currency too, gardens don't have to be instant. Let yours grow with you. One plant at a time is perfectly fine.

Create a Plan (or at least a Doodle)

Now comes the truly fun part, the imagining. You don't need a landscape architect's diploma. You just need curiosity, a notebook, and maybe a pair of coloured pencils.

• **Sketch your space**: Nothing fancy. Boxes and circles will do. Label areas; seating, pots, beds, paths. If you're the meticulous type (or just love stationery), dig out some graph paper and a ruler and draw your garden to scale. It's like being back at school but with more flowers and less algebra.

• **Mood board**: Clip ideas from magazines, print images, or create a Pinterest board. It helps you visualise and stay focused.

• **Wish list**: Favourite plants? Dream features? Start jotting them down. Be bold, write down a pergola even if you only have space for a pot. Dreams first, editing later.

• **Practicalities**: Where will your water butt go? Compost bin? Tool storage? These are the unsung heroes of garden planning and should get pride of place (even if it's behind a trellis).

Even the roughest plan gives you a starting point and helps stop that "Where do I begin?" feeling. And if you're not the sketching type, don't worry. Just make a list. This isn't a test; it's a vision.

Final Thoughts

Your garden sanctuary starts here, not with soil or seeds, but with intention. With a quiet moment to ask: What do I want from this space? Is it peace? Play? Produce? Privacy? You can have one, or all of the above. You just need to begin.

So grab your pen, your mug of tea, and your wildest garden dreams. No space is too small. No budget is too tight. Every garden, no matter how modest, has the potential to become something magical.

Next up: let's talk tools, the unsung heroes of your new green empire.

CHAPTER THREE

TOOLS

What to wield, when to wield it,

and how not to lose it in the compost

Before we get elbow-deep in soil, let's talk tools. The right ones make all the difference between a blissful gardening session and a frustrating game of "what can I use to dig this hole besides a spoon?" Now, I'm not suggesting you need a shed full of shiny, top-shelf gadgets that look like they belong in a Bond film. Just a sensible selection of trusty companions—your gardening Avengers, if you will.

The Big Three: Spade, Fork and Trowel

These are your ride-or-die garden tools. Without them, it's all a bit of a dig-and-hope affair.

• **Spade**: The heavyweight champion. Use it for digging, turning soil, edging beds, and shifting compost. Go for one with a strong handle and a blade that suits your height—your back will thank you.

• **Fork**: Excellent for loosening compacted soil, breaking up clumps, and working in compost or fertiliser. Ideal for heavy clay soil and autumn digging.

• **Trowel**: Think of it as your soil scalpel. Perfect for planting seedlings, scooping compost, or removing weeds from tight corners.

Tip: Stainless steel blades glide through soil like a hot knife through butter and are easier to clean. Wooden handles add that classic touch (and stop your hands freezing).

Support Squad: Other Handy Essentials

These are the tools that may not make headlines, but trust me, you'll find yourself reaching for them more often than you'd expect.

• **Watering Can**: Go for one with a detachable rose for gentle showers over seedlings. Choose a size you can carry comfortably— water is heavier than it looks, especially when you're trying not to spill it on your shoes.

• **Gloves**: Get a few pairs—tough ones for thorny jobs, and soft flexible ones for delicate work like potting. Bonus: clean fingernails and fewer surprises under them later.

• **Hand Fork**: Brilliant for surface weeding, especially in containers or raised beds. It's like giving your soil a light fluff with a very small pitchfork.

• **Secateurs**: Your everyday snips for deadheading, pruning, and taming unruly stems. A sharp, comfortable pair is worth every penny. Blunt secateurs are the gardening equivalent of a butter knife in a steakhouse.

• **Loppers**: Like secateurs, but on steroids. Perfect for thicker branches or shrubs that have delusions of grandeur. They're the go-to when your secateurs give up.

• **Hoe**: Excellent for tackling weeds before they even think about flowering. A Dutch hoe with a flat blade makes quick work of large areas and saves your back.

• **Kneeling Pad**: Your knees are precious—treat them like royalty. A squishy pad (or even a foam yoga block in disguise) can turn a crouch into a luxury experience.

• **Compost Scoop**: Larger and deeper than a trowel, this makes shifting compost from bag to pot a breeze. Less spilling, less swearing.

• **Notebook or Plant Journal**: Essential for keeping track of what you've planted, where, and when. Add sketches, lists, or even the odd poetic thought. It's your garden's diary—and future you will thank you for it.

• **Garden Knife**: A multi-purpose miracle. Cut string, divide perennials, open compost bags, trim back foliage. Keep it sharp and don't let it wander off into the kitchen drawer.

Plant Ties: Gentle Persuasion for Wayward Stems

Sometimes, plants need a little nudge in the right direction. Plant ties are your friendly plant whisperers.

• **Soft ties**: Velcro, rubber-coated wire, or padded twist ties; they hold firmly but gently.

• **Garden twine**: The classic. Simple, compostable, and endlessly handy.

• **Repurposed items**: Bits of string, old tights, shoelaces (ideally clean and not currently in service).

Just remember: you're supporting, not strangling. Always leave a little wiggle room—plants, like people, grow better when they're not being choked.

Containers: Home Sweet Home for Roots

Not all plants want to live in the ground, and not all gardeners have it to spare. Containers give you flexibility, creativity, and often, a stylish touch.

• **Terracotta pots**: These classic clay containers are porous, allowing air and water to pass through the walls—great for root health. Their warm, earthy look suits most garden styles, but beware: they're heavy when full and can crack in frosty weather, so

• **Plastic pots**: Lightweight, affordable, and durable. They retain moisture better than terracotta and are easy to move around, making them ideal for changing displays. Look for recycled or recyclable plastic options—some are now made from post-consumer waste and still look great.

• **Wooden planters**: Great for larger displays like mini trees or floral arrangements. They add natural charm and can blend into more rustic or classic garden styles. To prolong their life, line the inside with plastic (poke holes for drainage) and raise them slightly off the ground.

• **Fabric grow bags**: These breathable, foldable wonders are perfect for temporary gardens or growing crops like potatoes, salad leaves, or even dahlias. They allow good drainage and air circulation to the roots, helping prevent rot and encouraging vigorous growth. Just remember to water more frequently.

• **Upcycled items**: This is where you get to flex your creative muscles. Old drawers, colanders, teapots, baskets—even boots—can become unique homes for plants. Just ensure they have drainage holes and are positioned where they'll get the right amount of sun or shade. Bonus points if it makes a guest say, "Wait, is that a bread bin full of begonias?"

Remember: drainage is key. No one likes soggy roots.

Storage Solutions: Tools Need Homes Too

A well-organised space makes gardening feel like joy, not a treasure hunt.

Tool sheds or lockers: Weatherproof and practical.

Hooks and hanging racks: Great for sheds, garages, or outdoor walls.

Totes or trugs: For moving tools around with ease. Stylish ones even double as décor.**Upcycled furniture:** Old bookshelves or dressers make charming storage spots.

Keep a small toolkit in an easily accessible basket or box, especially helpful for quick after-work gardening sessions.

A Few Words on Quality If you can, invest in tools that feel good in your hand and are built to last. Quality doesn't always mean pricey, but flimsiness almost always ends in frustration. Ask yourself: does it feel sturdy? Comfortable? Is it rust-resistant? If yes; buy it, name it, cherish it.

Final Thoughts

You don't need every tool under the sun to get started. A few key pieces, a good attitude, and a willingness to learn will get you further than a van full of gear. Begin with the essentials. Add as you grow. And remember, a seasoned gardener with a trowel and a smile can accomplish more than anyone armed with tech but no time.

Next up: let's talk about soil; the dark, mysterious magic beneath your boots.

CHAPTER FOUR

SOIL

The foundation of your garden sanctuary
(and your new best friend)

Ah, soil. The unsung hero of the garden. While flowers and foliage get all the glory, it's what's happening underfoot that truly matters. Think of soil as the backstage crew in a theatre production, largely invisible, entirely essential, and capable of making (or breaking) the show.

Before you plant a single petunia or sow a solitary seed, it's time to get your hands dirty, literally, and dig into the wild and wonderful world of soil. Don't worry, this isn't a dry science lesson. This is about understanding your garden from the ground up.

What is Soil, Really?

Let's bust a myth: soil is not just dirt. Dirt is what you vacuum. Soil is alive. It's a rich, complex mix of materials that support plant life and play host to a microcosmic world of organisms.

The Main Components of Soil

Mineral Particles (About 45%) These are sand, silt, and clay; the building blocks of soil texture. They originate from weathered rock and give soil its weight, structure, and drainage properties.

Sand is coarse and gritty, drains quickly, and warms up fast.

Silt feels smooth like flour, holds moisture well, and is more fertile than sand.

Clay is fine and sticky when wet, slow to drain, and holds onto nutrients like a miser.

Organic Matter (Around 5%) This includes decomposed plant and animal material, also known as humus. It improves soil structure, retains moisture, and provides a steady food source for microorganisms and plants. Compost, leaf mould, and manure all add to this rich resource.

Water (Approx. 25%) Held in the spaces between soil particles, water is essential for transporting nutrients to plant roots. The balance between too much (waterlogged) and too little (parched) depends on your soil texture.

Air (Approx. 25%) Oxygen is vital, not just for roots, but for the billions of tiny organisms living underground. Well-aerated soil supports root development and microbial activity.

Microorganisms (Tiny but Mighty) These include bacteria, fungi, protozoa, nematodes, and the ever-adorable earthworms. They break down organic material, convert nutrients into forms plants can absorb, and keep soil ecosystems humming along.

Your soil isn't just a medium, it's a living, breathing ecosystem. Treat it with respect, and it will reward you generously.

Soil Composition and Texture

The Soil Triangle: Sand, Silt, and Clay
Soil texture refers to the proportion of these three mineral particles in your soil.

Sand: Largest particle size; feels gritty. Excellent drainage, poor nutrient retention.

Silt: Medium-sized particles; feels silky. Holds moisture better and has decent fertility.

Clay: Tiny particles; feels sticky and heavy. Great at holding nutrients, but can become compacted and poorly drained.

The texture of your soil affects everything from drainage and fertility to how easy it is to dig. Most garden soils contain a mix of all three types, and the balance of each determines its texture category.

Loam: The Gold Standard

Loam is the ideal blend of all three:

40%sand
40%silt
20% clay

This mixture offers the best of all worlds; good drainage, excellent fertility, and a soft, crumbly texture that's easy to work with. Loam holds moisture and nutrients without becoming soggy or compacted. If your soil isn't naturally loamy, don't panic, this chapter will help you get closer to that happy balance.

Soil Structure

Structure refers to how soil particles group together. These clusters, called aggregates, determine the soil's ability to retain water, support roots, and resist erosion.

• **Granular (like breadcrumbs)**: Loose, well-formed structure common in loamy or organically rich soils. Easy for roots to push through and great for water infiltration.

• **Blocky or Platy**: Dense, hard-to-break chunks. Can occur in clay-heavy soils or areas that have been compacted. Water struggles to move through, and roots do too.

• **Compact**: A worst-case scenario. Occurs in overworked or poorly maintained soil. It's like trying to garden in a brick.

Improving soil structure is all about adding organic matter, avoiding over-tilling, and letting nature (earthworms, microbes, fungi) do the hard work.

How to Test Your Soil

Understanding your soil's quirks is the first step to working with it, not against it.

The Jar Test

A fun kitchen experiment:

Fill a clear jar with soil (about one-third full).Top it up with water, shake well, and let it settle overnight.

Layers will form: sand at the bottom, silt in the middle, clay on top.

This gives you a visual breakdown of your soil's texture.

The Squeeze Test

Grab a handful of damp soil and give it a squeeze:

Falls apart? Sandy.

Forms a ball but crumbles with poking? Loamy.

Stays in a stubborn lump? Clay.

pH Testing

Soil pH affects nutrient availability and plant health. Most plants prefer a pH between 6.0 and 7.0 (slightly acidic to neutral).

Use a home testing kit or send a sample to a lab.

Acidic soil (pH < 6): Suits azaleas, rhododendrons, blueberries.

Alkaline soil (pH > 7): Great for lavender, lilacs, clematis.

Adjust pH with lime (to raise it) or sulphur (to lower it), but go gently. Gradual changes are best.

Organic Matter: The Gardener's Gold

Adding organic matter is the single best thing you can do for your soil.

Why it Matters:

Improves soil structure

Increases water retention

Feeds soil life

Encourages root development

Sources of Organic Matter

Compost: Kitchen and garden waste transformed into black gold.

Well-rotted manure: From herbivores only (no cat or dog waste).

Leaf mould: Fallen leaves turned into rich humus.

Green manure: Crops grown to be dug back into the soil.

Mulch: Straw, bark, or grass clippings that break down over time.

A yearly top-dressing of organic matter is like a spa treatment for your soil. It makes everything feel better.

Soil for Containers

If you're gardening in pots, your soil situation is slightly different. You're in full control, hooray! But it also means you need to supply everything the plant needs.

Use a good-quality potting mix, ideally peat-free.

Add perlite or vermiculite for drainage.

Mix in slow-release fertiliser or compost.

Container soil can compact over time; refresh it yearly by removing the top layer and topping up with fresh compost.

Soil and Drainage

Waterlogged soil leads to root rot and unhappy plants. Test your drainage:

Dig a hole about 30cm deep, fill it with water.

If it drains within an hour: great.

If it takes longer than two hours, poor drainage.

Improve it by adding organic matter, installing drainage channels, or creating raised beds.

Encouraging Soil Life

Healthy soil is teeming with life. Encourage this underground party with good practices:

Avoid chemical fertilisers and pesticides, they kill helpful organisms.

Mulch regularly to keep soil moist and fed.

Grow cover crops in winter to prevent erosion and feed microbes.

Plant a variety of species to support biodiversity.

Worms are a great sign; nature's tiny tillers, constantly aerating your soil

.

No-Dig Gardening The no-dig approach is gaining popularity for good reason. It protects soil structure and nurtures the soil food web.

Add compost and mulch on top of the soil.

Let worms and microbes do the digging for you.

Less weeding, less watering, more life below ground.

Especially ideal for raised beds and low-maintenance plots.

Regional Soil Considerations

Let's take a closer look at what you're likely to find underfoot depending on where you are, because despite the British love of complaining about our weather, our soil types are as varied as our accents.

UK Soil Types

Clay Soil: Yes, the classic. Found in many parts of southern and central England. It holds nutrients brilliantly but drains slowly and can turn into concrete in summer. Great for: roses, asters, and fruit trees, if you improve the drainage.

Sandy Soil: More common in the southeast and coastal areas. Fast-draining and warms up quickly in spring, but needs lots of organic matter to hold nutrients. Great for: lavender, rosemary, carrots, and beetroot.

Silty Soil: Found in low-lying regions and near rivers, like the Fens. Rich in nutrients and moisture-retentive, but prone to compaction. Great for: grasses, shrubs, and most vegetables.

Peaty Soil: Mostly found in Scotland, parts of Wales, and moorland areas. Dark, spongy, acidic, and moisture-rich. Great for: heathers, azaleas, camellias, and blueberries.

Chalky Soil: Common in the South Downs and parts of Wiltshire. Alkaline and stony with good drainage, but not great at holding water. Great for: lilacs, dianthus, and clematis.

Loam Soil: The jackpot. Found in pockets across the country and often sold in garden centres. Balanced and versatile. Great for... well, almost everything.

No matter your patch, soil can be improved with love, mulch, and compost. But knowing your starting point helps you choose plants that'll thrive rather than merely survive.

US Zones

Southeast (Florida, Georgia): Sandy soils with organic matter on top; drain well but need feeding.

Southwest (Arizona, New Mexico): Dry, alkaline soils that need mulching and moisture retention.

Northeast (New York, Pennsylvania): Often loamy with decent organic content, good for most crops.

Midwest (Illinois, Ohio): Rich prairie soils, but clay-heavy in urban areas.

Pacific Northwest (Oregon, Washington): High organic content and moisture, ideal for lush gardens.

Wherever you are, you're not stuck with "bad soil," you're simply starting a relationship with your specific patch of earth. The aim is progress, not perfection.

Get to know your garden's unique environment. Local extension services or gardening groups can provide regional advice.

Common Soil Problems (and Fixes)

Problem	Cause	Solution
Cracked, dry soil	Too much clay, compacted	Add compost, mulch, avoid overwatering
Yellowing plants	Poor drainage or pH imbalance	Test soil, adjust watering or pH
Slow growth	Lack of nutrients	Add organic matter, rotate crops
Moss or algae	Poor drainage, acidic pH	Improve aeration, adjust soil conditions

Final Thoughts

If gardening is an act of love, then soil is where that love takes root. Learn to listen to it. Observe it. Feed it. Protect it. Soil is not just the starting point of your garden; it's its lifeblood.

Take the time to understand your soil, and you'll find that everything else; plant health, blooms, harvests, joy, flows more easily. Think of it as a partnership. The more you give, the more you'll grow.

Next up, we're reaching for the skies, let's talk vertical gardening!

CHAPTER FIVE

HEIGHT

Vertical gardening for
small spaces and
ambitious plants

Let's be honest, gardening can feel a bit greedy for space. And if your plot is roughly the size of a picnic blanket, you might think your green-fingered dreams are out of reach. But fear not, for there is a magical direction yet to explore: **up**. Vertical gardening is your new best friend. It's the ultimate trick to squeezing lushness out of lean spaces. Think of it as the garden world's equivalent of a clever updo; practical, pretty, and positively chic.

Honestly, it's a bit like giving your garden a facelift. Suddenly everything looks perkier, bouncier, and far more intentional. It's all about making the most of what you've got, especially if what you've got is less Downton Abbey and more 'two-pots-and-a-dream' kind of garden.

Ideal Supports: Trellises, Felt Walls, and All Things Upright

Welcome to the architectural department of your vertical paradise, where function meets flair and even the humblest of peas can rise to lofty heights. When it comes to vertical gardening, your support structures are the stage, and your plants? Well, they're the stars giving an Oscar-worthy performance.

Trellises

The dependable best friend of the climbing world. Whether it's made of wood, metal, or something crafty and homemade, a trellis gives your garden instant structure and your plants something to cling to like a tipsy aunt at a wedding.

Wooden Trellises: Ideal for cottage-style gardens, they bring warmth and a rustic charm. Pair with sweet peas, roses, or honeysuckle for that full Beatrix Potter fantasy.

Metal Trellises: Sleek, strong, and modern. Think city chic with clematis and jasmine twirling their way skyward in a stylish embrace.

Foldable Trellises: Great for small-space dwellers or renters. They can be propped up when needed and folded away like a deckchair after a British summer barbecue.

Top tip: Angle them slightly away from walls to allow airflow and to keep leaves from getting too snuggly with brickwork (hello, mildew).

Obelisks and Arches

When your plants are feeling dramatic and let's face it, many of them are, these are your go-to glamour supports.

Obelisks: Tall, pyramidal, and proud. Pop one in the centre of a raised bed or large container for a true showstopper moment. Sweet peas, climbing nasturtiums, or black-eyed Susan vines will oblige with a flourish.

Arches: Create a natural doorway to enchantment. Whether draped in roses, honeysuckle, or clematis, arches are the garden's equivalent of rolling out the red carpet.

Bonus: They make excellent selfie spots. Just saying

Felt Pocket Walls

Imagine a vertical organiser for your plants like a hanging shoe rack, but greener and with fewer smelly trainers. These felt walls are perfect for compact growing and city balconies that dream of countryside charm.

Ideal for light-rooted plants like violas, lobelia, and trailing petunias.

Keep them well-watered, felt dries out faster than a sponge in the Sahara.

Group plants with similar light and moisture needs to keep everyone happy. No divas allowed.

Tip: They're brilliant for seasonal swaps, just replant fresh blooms as the year rolls on.

Wire Frames and Mesh Panels

Simple, practical, and DIY-friendly. A roll of mesh or a repurposed panel can transform a dull fence into a green tapestry.

Zip-tie them to anything vaguely upright; balconies, walls, trellis bases.

Paint them black or sage green for a cleaner look or let them rust romantically if you're into that sort of thing.

Perfect for annual climbers or creating your own living green wall.

Great for budget gardeners or those with an eye for upcycling; old bed frames, anyone?

Hanging Baskets and Wall-Mounted Planters

Whimsy, thy name is hanging basket. These dangling delights are perfect for injecting joy, movement, and colour at eye level (and above).

Choose trailing plants with personality; think bacopa, ivy-leaf geraniums, or fuchsias that drip like chandelier earrings.

Use baskets in odd numbers for visual rhythm and avoid hanging them where they'll bonk unsuspecting guests in the forehead.

Mix flowering plants with cascading foliage for texture or go monochrome for a chic minimalist vibe.

Just make sure everything is securely fixed. Nothing says "welcome to my sanctuary" like a falling pot of begonias landing squarely on the patio.

Climbers and Creepers

These are the natural-born mountaineers of the plant world. They love to climb up trellises, obelisks, wires, or walls, and many bring scent, colour, and personality in spades.

Clematis: Comes in many shapes, sizes, and blooming seasons, from delicate spring varieties like 'Montana' to bold summer-flowering 'Jackmanii'. Needs its roots shaded and head in the sun.

Sweet Peas (Lathyrus odoratus): Scented, colourful, and romantic. Ideal for arches and wigwams. Deadhead regularly for more blooms.

Climbing Roses: Such as 'Zephirine Drouhin' or 'New Dawn', bring a burst of colour and scent. Train them along walls or over pergolas.

Star Jasmine (Trachelospermum jasminoides): Evergreen, highly fragrant in summer, and great for sunny, sheltered spots.

Passiflora (Passionflower): Exotic-looking blooms and rapid growth. Great for a tropical feel.

Wisteria: A classic for pergolas and facades. Produces breathtaking cascades of lilac or white in late spring. Needs sturdy support and regular pruning.

Honeysuckle (Lonicera): Attracts pollinators with sweet fragrance and tubular flowers. Perfect for softening a fence.

Climbing Hydrangea (Hydrangea anomala petiolaris): Slow to get going but rewards you with lush foliage and lace-like flowers. Self-clinging.

Akebia quinata (Chocolate Vine): Fast-growing, semi-evergreen, with unusual maroon flowers and a sweet scent.

Ivy (Hedera helix): Tough, evergreen, and good for year-round cover but give it boundaries or it will stage a coup.

Spillers and Fillers

These plants are great for softening edges, filling pockets, or cascading down from baskets and containers. Use them to add volume and whimsy to any vertical setup.

Lobelia ('Cascade' types): Masses of tiny, vibrant blue or purple flowers that trail beautifully from hanging baskets.

Trailing Petunias (Surfinia): Long, colourful cascades that bloom for months with regular **feeding.**

Fuchsias: Best for part-shade, these classic draping plants add elegance and colour. Look for varieties like 'Swingtime' or 'Southgate'.

Verbena (Trailing types): Bright, bee-friendly flowers with a trailing habit. Lovely in window boxes.

Bacopa: Small, profuse white or lavender flowers. Low-maintenance and excellent for filling gaps.

Calibrachoa ('Million Bells'): Like miniature petunias, these come in a rainbow of colours and are wonderfully prolific.

Dichondra 'Silver Falls': A cool-toned trailing foliage plant with shimmering silver leaves. Great for contrast.

Campanula ('Trailing Bellflower'): Starry flowers in purple or white. Good for shady pockets.

Begonia (trailing types): Ideal for shade and moist conditions. Produces showy blooms in hanging containers.

Helichrysum petiolare: Soft, felted leaves with a flowing habit. Pairs beautifully with brighter flowers in mixed arrangements.

Fast Growers and Show-Offs

Impatient? These plants will fill your vertical space in no time, bringing instant impact and seasonal cheer.

Morning Glory (Ipomoea): Fast and fabulous. Twisting vines and eye-popping colour, ideal for trellises.

Black-eyed Susan Vine (Thunbergia alata): Quick climber with sunny yellow or orange flowers and a dark centre.

Nasturtiums (Trailing types): Cheery, fast-growing flowers with large leaves and generous blooms; though not for eating here!

Canary Creeper (Tropaeolum peregrinum): Delicate, fringed yellow flowers on long, climbing stems. Looks like a vine in motion.

Cobaea scandens (Cup and Saucer Vine): Bold purple bell-shaped flowers and glossy leaves. Vigorous and dramatic.

Eccremocarpus scaber (Chilean Glory Flower): A lesser-known gem with tubular, fiery flowers. Loved by hummingbirds and humans alike.

Lathyrus latifolius (Perennial Sweet Pea): No scent, but tough as nails and blooms through summer.

Tropaeolum speciosum (Flame Nasturtium): A bit finicky, but with spectacular red blooms over fine foliage when happy.

Ipomoea lobata (Spanish Flag): A fast climber with red-to-yellow gradient flowers. Great for wow-factor.

Asarina scandens (Twining Snapdragon): Delicate vines with snapdragon-like flowers in jewel tones.

A Few Quick Tips Before You Go Vertical

Watering: Vertical setups can dry out faster. Install drip irrigation or make a habit of daily check-ins (plants love attention).

Weight Matters: Don't overload your structures, check they're secure and can bear the botanical weight.

Sunlight Strategy: Tall plants can cast shade. Be strategic with placement so everyone gets their moment in the sun.

Feeding: Container-based vertical systems need regular feeding. Liquid seaweed is brilliant.

Regular Checks: Tie in climbers as they grow, check for pests, and deadhead for longer blooming. It's like haircare, but with snails.

Seasonal Swaps and Ever-Changing Walls One of the joys of vertical gardening is the ability to change things up with the seasons:

Spring: Plant violas, pansies, snapdragons, and salad greens.

Summer: Let petunias, nasturtiums, and tomatoes take the stage.

Autumn: Add ornamental cabbage, trailing ivy, and autumn cyclamen.

Winter: Switch to evergreens, heathers, and wall-hardy herbs like thyme.

Your vertical garden can evolve throughout the year like a living tapestry.

Creative Combos and Design Ideas

Colour themes: Try a purple wall (lavender, petunias, salvia) or a white-and-green combo for a calming vibe. For white and green, consider white bacopa, white trailing lobelia, snowy alyssum, variegated ivy, Dusty Miller, and silver dichondra; cool, elegant, and effortlessly stylish.

Texture play: Mix upright spikes (like verbena, salvia, or snapdragons) with tumbling trailers such as bacopa, calibrachoa, dichondra 'Silver Falls', or creeping Jenny. Contrast fluffy blooms with glossy foliage or fine grasses with soft-leaved begonias.

Vertical herb spiral: Create a spiral structure from bricks or wood and plant with your favourite herbs.

Pallet garden: Lay a wooden pallet flat, fill it with soil and plants, then stand it upright. Boom. Instant wall.

Final Thoughts

Vertical gardening is proof that great things come in small (and tall) packages. Whether you're working with a teeny courtyard, a sunny balcony, or just a corner of a patio, the sky really is the limit. And between us, it's *ridiculously* satisfying watching your garden climb.

So go on, let your plants rise to the occasion. Throw in a few cheeky climbers, hang up your hanging baskets with pride, and stand back as your sanctuary grows skyward. Upwards, green soldier, and onward to glory!

Next up: plant selection through the seasons, because gardens don't just bloom in June!

CHAPTER SIX

PLANTS

What to plant and when,
from snowdrops to sunflowers

One of the great joys of creating a garden sanctuary is watching it shift and shimmy with the seasons, each bringing its own unique palette, scent, and energy. With a bit of planning (and a dash of plant matchmaking), you can ensure that your little slice of paradise has something going on all year round. No bare patches. No seasonal sadness. Just a continuous cycle of colour, texture, and "ooh look, that's blooming now!"

Let's break it down season by season so your garden becomes a year-round source of delight and the envy of neighbours on both sides. Each section will cover key flowers, perennials, shrubs, and annuals, along with their best planting times and how to combine them for maximum impact.

Spring: The Garden Wakes Up (and So Do You)

Spring is the season of awakening. The soil softens, the light lengthens, and the garden begins to stir with a quiet kind of electricity. Buds swell on bare stems, poised like tiny promises, and last year's twigs suddenly remember their job, pushing out green tips like they've never stopped trying. There's something deeply moving about those first signs of life, watching a seedling break through the soil, all elbows and optimism, or catching the sunlight on a daffodil that wasn't there yesterday. Even the weeds arrive with enthusiasm, as if everyone got the memo: it's time to grow. Bees bumble out, a little confused at first, while birds seem to gossip louder in the warming air. It's a season of hope, bright greens, and gentle colour when the whole garden exhales and whispers, *"We're back."*

What to Expect in Spring

Early Blooms for Instant Cheer The first flowers of the season feel like a standing ovation after a long, grey performance of winter.

Snowdrops, crocuses, and daffodils peek out with bold optimism, scattering brightness like nature's confetti. These early risers lift spirits and signal that, yes, better (and warmer) days are coming.

Blossoms and Bulbs Galore From tulips in pots to hyacinths along the borders, spring is a bulb-fuelled bonanza. Trees burst into clouds of blossom, with cherry, magnolia, and flowering currant turning gardens into pastel wonderlands. Every corner feels like it's been kissed by a watercolour brush dipped in blush pink and soft lavender.

Fresh, Lime-Green Foliage Everywhere There's a very particular shade of green that only spring can produce; zesty, tender, and full of promise. It unfurls slowly on hedges, perennials, and shrubs, giving your garden the glow of something freshly awakened. You might even catch yourself stroking a new leaf like it's a baby lamb. (Go on. We all do it.)

Flowering Bulbs and Perennials

Plant Name	Type	Description	When to Plant
Daffodils (Narcissus)	Bulb	Bright yellow or white trumpet-shaped flowers; early season cheer	Autumn (Sept–Nov)
Tulips	Bulb	Come in nearly every colour; great for containers and borders	Autumn (Oct–Nov)
Bluebells (Hyacinthoides non-scripta)	Bulb	A beloved UK spring classic; naturalised in woodlands, with elegant violet-blue flowers	Autumn (Sept–Nov)
Crocus	Bulb	Dainty early bloomers; perfect for naturalising lawns	Autumn (Sept–Nov)
Hyacinths	Bulb	Scented and compact with pastel blooms	Autumn (Sept–Nov)
Hellebores	Perennial	Winter-to-spring bloomers; subtle and elegant	Autumn or early spring
Pulmonaria	Perennial	Spotted foliage and pink/blue flowers; great for shade	Autumn or early spring
Brunnera	Perennial	Heart-shaped leaves and blue forget-me-not-like flowers	Spring
Primroses (Primula vulgaris)	Perennial	Soft yellow blooms in shady spots; a true sign of British springtime	Autumn

Layer bulbs in containers: Think of it as a floral lasagne, each layer timed to bloom in succession for a long-lasting spring show. Start with **daffodils** at the bottom (they're the tallest and take the longest to grow), planting them about 20cm (8 inches) deep. Add a layer of compost, then position your **tulips** about 10–15cm (4–6 inches) deep. Finish with **crocus** near the top, just 5–8cm (2–3 inches) deep. Cover with compost, water in, and wait. You'll be rewarded with a cascade of blooms; crocus first, then tulips, and finally daffodils, all from one seemingly magical pot. Choose varieties with staggered flowering times to keep the colour coming.

Shrubs and Trees

Plant Name	Type	Description	When to Plant
Forsythia	Shrub	Bright yellow blooms on bare branches	Autumn to early spring
Camellia	Shrub	Evergreen with glossy leaves and rose-like flowers	Autumn
Flowering Currant (Ribes)	Shrub	Rosy-pink flowers, loved by pollinators	Autumn or spring
Magnolia	Shrub/Tree	Large showy flowers; pink, white or purple	Autumn or spring

Summer: The Garden in Full Song Summer is the garden's party season; everything bursts into full performance mode, from ruffled roses to flouncy salvias. The colours deepen, the scents grow heady, and the borders hum with bees like nature's own jazz band. Plants strut their stuff like it's the Chelsea Flower Show every day and they've just had a professional blow-dry. This is the season of garden pride, when your earlier planning pays off and your sanctuary starts showing off a bit (and rightly so). It's also the time when keeping on top of watering, feeding, and deadheading turns into a strangely satisfying ritual; equal parts maintenance and meditation.

What to Expect in Summer: Rich, saturated colour that practically sings Summer doesn't tiptoe in, it struts. Borders burst into technicolour with blazing reds, electric purples, sunshine yellows, and every glorious hue in between. It's like nature raided the crayon box and said, "More is more."

• **Fragrance that intensifies with heat; lavender, roses, and honeysuckle at their most dramatic** This is scent season. As the temperature rises, your garden turns into an open-air perfume counter. Lavender hums in the heat, old-fashioned roses exhale deep floral notes, and honeysuckle drapes itself over arches with sweet abandon. Step outside and inhale deeply, it's therapy with petals.

• **An abundance of pollinators, fluttering, buzzing, and generally throwing a garden rave** Every flower seems to come with its own entourage of guests: bees stumbling drunkenly from bloom to bloom, butterflies fluttering like gossiping aunties, and hoverflies doing aerial ballet. It's a joyful, buzzing sign that your garden is working exactly as it should.

• **A riot of texture, height, and movement, this is no time for subtlety** Tall spires sway in the breeze, delicate fronds shimmer in the light, and dense foliage creates contrast and drama. Everything's growing like it's had three cups of coffee and a pep talk. There's energy in the air, and your plants are absolutely feeling it.

Summer Bulbs

Plant Name	Description	When to Plant
Dahlias	From dinner-plate to pom-pom forms, they bring late-summer brilliance.	Spring (after frost)
Lilies (Asiatic/Oriental)	Tall, elegant, often fragrant; perfect in borders or pots.	Spring
Gladiolus	Towering spires in bold colours, ideal for cutting gardens.	Spring
Crocosmia (Montbretia)	Arching stems and fiery flowers that scream summer.	Spring
Allium sphaerocephalon	Later-blooming drumstick alliums are quirky and bee-friendly.	Autumn
Galtonia (Summer Hyacinth)	Tall spires of nodding white bells. Underused and lovely.	Spring
Eucomis (Pineapple Lily)	Unique structure; ideal for containers.	Spring
Tigridia (Tiger Flower)	Tropical look, short-lived blooms, but striking.	Spring
Calla Lily (Zantedeschia)	Graceful, architectural, ideal for damp soil or pots.	Spring
Acidanthera	Elegant white flowers with a dark centre and a rich fragrance.	Spring
Begonia (tuberous)	Shade-loving and brilliant for hanging baskets or window boxes.	Spring
Freesia	Delicate, perfumed flowers, lovely in pots and small beds.	Spring

Gloriosa Lily	Exotic climber for pots in warm spots (or indoors in cooler zones).	Spring (indoors)
Ixia	Star-shaped flowers, ideal in sunny borders.	Autumn or Spring
Sparaxis (Harlequin Flower)	Rainbow-bright and full of summer joy.	Autumn or Spring

Summer Shrubs (including Fragrant Roses)

These bring structure, repeat blooms, and lush scents that linger in warm air.

Plant Name	Description	When to Plant
Rosa 'Gertrude Jekyll'	Strong, old rose scent; rich pink blooms.	Autumn or early spring
Rosa 'Lady Emma Hamilton'	Citrus fragrance and tangerine-pink colour.	Autumn or early spring
Rosa 'Madame Alfred Carrière'	Climbing, pale blush blooms with a rich perfume.	Autumn or early spring
Lavender (Angustifolia, Hidcote)	Compact, fragrant, and pollinator gold.	Spring
Hydrangea paniculata 'Limelight'	Lime-to-cream cones; great in part shade.	Autumn or early spring
Buddleja davidii (Butterfly Bush)	Every garden should have one, scented and alive with butterflies.	Autumn or early spring
Philadelphus (Mock Orange)	Powerful orange blossom scent in early summer.	Autumn or early spring
Deutzia	Clusters of tiny white or pink blooms; good filler shrub.	Autumn or early spring
Potentilla fruticosa	Long-blooming, cheerful shrubs in yellow, white, or pink.	Spring or autumn
Caryopteris (Bluebeard)	Compact, blue-flowered, and adored by bees.	Spring or autumn

Choisya ternata (Mexican Orange Blossom)	Glossy foliage and citrus-scented flowers.	Spring or autumn
Spiraea japonica	Soft pink blooms and tidy form.	Spring or autumn
Hypericum (St. John's Wort)	Bright yellow blooms with red berries in autumn.	Spring or autumn
Abelia x grandiflora	Semi-evergreen with long-lasting blooms and fragrance.	Autumn or early spring
Rosa 'The Generous Gardener'	Pale pink climber, highly scented and repeat-blooming.	Autumn or early spring

Summer Perennials

Reliable and often long-flowering, these return year after year for glorious midsummer displays.

Plant Name	Description	When to Plant
Salvia nemorosa	Spikes of violet or blue that hum with bees.	Spring or autumn
Echinacea purpurea (Coneflower)	Sturdy, daisy-like flowers in bold colours.	Spring or autumn
Penstemon	Tubular flowers and long blooming period.	Spring
Coreopsis	Sun-loving and generous bloomers.	Spring
Gaura lindheimeri	Airy, delicate flowers that flutter in the breeze.	Spring
Shasta Daisy (Leucanthemum)	Cheerful, white blooms with sunny centres.	Spring
Scabiosa (Pincushion Flower)	Textural, pastel-toned, and great in borders.	Spring or autumn
Achillea (Yarrow)	Flat-headed clusters in warm hues; pollinator favourite.	Spring
Phlox paniculata	Tall, fragrant, and good for cutting.	Spring or autumn
Veronica spicata (Speedwell)	Low clumps with vertical flower spikes.	Spring
Monarda (Bee Balm)	Wild, frizzy blooms and minty-scented foliage.	Spring

Rudbeckia fulgida (Black-eyed Susan)	Late summer rays of yellow with dark centres.	Spring or autumn
Kniphofia (Red Hot Poker)	Bold, upright, and a touch exotic.	Spring
Helenium (Sneezeweed)	Warm colours and reliable performance.	Spring
Campanula (Bellflower)	Purple or white, excellent ground cover or upright.	Spring or autumn

Summer Annuals

Perfect for quick colour, containers, and creating a joyful, ever-changing display.

Plant Name	Description	When to Plant
Salvia nemorosa	Spikes of violet or blue that hum with bees.	Spring or autumn
Echinacea purpurea (Coneflower)	Sturdy, daisy-like flowers in bold colours.	Spring or autumn
Penstemon	Tubular flowers and long blooming period.	Spring
Coreopsis	Sun-loving and generous bloomers.	Spring
Gaura lindheimeri	Airy, delicate flowers that flutter in the breeze.	Spring
Shasta Daisy (Leucanthemum)	Cheerful, white blooms with sunny centres.	Spring
Scabiosa (Pincushion Flower)	Textural, pastel-toned, and great in borders.	Spring or autumn
Achillea (Yarrow)	Flat-headed clusters in warm hues; pollinator favourite.	Spring
Phlox paniculata	Tall, fragrant, and good for cutting.	Spring or autumn
Veronica spicata (Speedwell)	Low clumps with vertical flower spikes.	Spring
Monarda (Bee Balm)	Wild, frizzy blooms and minty-scented foliage.	Spring

Rudbeckia fulgida (Black-eyed Susan)	Late summer rays of yellow with dark centres.	Spring or autumn
Kniphofia (Red Hot Poker)	Bold, upright, and a touch exotic.	Spring
Helenium (Sneezeweed)	Warm colours and reliable performance.	Spring
Campanula (Bellflower)	Purple or white, excellent ground cover or upright.	Spring or autumn

Climbers & Trailers (for Summer Impact)

The stars of vertical drama and living walls. Let them sprawl, climb, and cascade.

Plant Name	Description	When to Plant
Salvia nemorosa	Spikes of violet or blue that hum with bees.	Spring or autumn
Echinacea purpurea (Coneflower)	Sturdy, daisy-like flowers in bold colours.	Spring or autumn
Penstemon	Tubular flowers and long blooming period.	Spring
Coreopsis	Sun-loving and generous bloomers.	Spring
Gaura lindheimeri	Airy, delicate flowers that flutter in the breeze.	Spring
Shasta Daisy (Leucanthemum)	Cheerful, white blooms with sunny centres.	Spring
Scabiosa (Pincushion Flower)	Textural, pastel-toned, and great in borders.	Spring or autumn
Achillea (Yarrow)	Flat-headed clusters in warm hues; pollinator favourite.	Spring
Phlox paniculata	Tall, fragrant, and good for cutting.	Spring or autumn
Veronica spicata (Speedwell)	Low clumps with vertical flower spikes.	Spring
Monarda (Bee Balm)	Wild, frizzy blooms and minty-scented foliage.	Spring

Rudbeckia fulgida (Black-eyed Susan)	Late summer rays of yellow with dark centres.	Spring or autumn
Kniphofia (Red Hot Poker)	Bold, upright, and a touch exotic.	Spring
Helenium (Sneezeweed)	Warm colours and reliable performance.	Spring
Campanula (Bellflower)	Purple or white, excellent ground cover or upright.	Spring or autumn

Autumn/Fall: The Golden Glow

Autumn *or fall*, if you prefer your leaves with a transatlantic accent, is often billed as the garden's wind-down act, but in truth, it's more of a spectacular encore. This is the season when your garden puts on its most theatrical display. Trees and shrubs burst into flames of crimson, copper, and gold, borders glow with the final hurrah of late-blooming perennials, and seed heads stand tall like tiny sculptures. There's a crispness in the air and a sense of deep, settling magic underfoot, as if the earth is tucking itself in, but not before one last brilliant performance.

Grasses sway like golden ribbons, ornamental leaves rustle dramatically with every breeze, and berries bead themselves along stems like nature's jewellery. It's a time for rich tones, moody lighting, and garden textures that beg to be touched. And the best part? This mellow season is also one of the best planting times of the year; cooler soil, still-warm sun, and fewer weeds to battle.

What to Expect in Autumn/Fall

• **A garden ablaze with colour; think golds, russets, burgundies, and every warm tone in between** It's as if the whole garden has decided to throw on its cosiest jumper and light a scented candle. Foliage flames into fiery golds and coppery reds, like embers catching in the wind. Even the fading blooms seem to glow with a last burst of pride before bowing out for winter.

• **Dried flower heads and swaying seedpods offering structure and gentle movement** There's a subtle beauty in what's left behind. Alliums turn into elegant globes of lace, hydrangeas fade into antique tones, and ornamental grasses sway like dancers in slow motion. It's textural, sculptural, and unexpectedly soulful.

• **A wildlife buffet of berries, hips, and hollow stems for overwintering insects and hungry birds** Rosehips gleam like rubies, ivy berries ripen into dark treats, and seedheads become tiny rest stops for feathered visitors. While we pull on mittens, the garden quietly feeds and shelters everything from blackbirds to sleepy ladybirds/ladybugs.

• **The joy of planting now for spring because autumn isn't the end, it's a preparation disguised in glory** This season is a master of disguise. While it looks like things are winding down, the real magic is happening underground. Tulips and daffodils are tucked in like bedtime stories, perennials are bedding down for a nap, and gardeners are quietly making promises to spring.

Autumn/Fall Perennials

Late bloomers, graceful fillers, and a few scene-stealers that bring warmth and structure as the days cool.

Plant Name	Description	When to Plant
Salvia nemorosa	Spikes of violet or blue that hum with bees.	Spring or autumn
Echinacea purpurea (Coneflower)	Sturdy, daisy-like flowers in bold colours.	Spring or autumn
Penstemon	Tubular flowers and long blooming period.	Spring

Coreopsis	Sun-loving and generous bloomers.	Spring
Gaura lindheimeri	Airy, delicate flowers that flutter in the breeze.	Spring
Shasta Daisy (Leucanthemum)	Cheerful, white blooms with sunny centres.	Spring
Scabiosa (Pincushion Flower)	Textural, pastel-toned, and great in borders.	Spring or autumn
Achillea (Yarrow)	Flat-headed clusters in warm hues; pollinator favourite.	Spring
Phlox paniculata	Tall, fragrant, and good for cutting.	Spring or autumn
Veronica spicata (Speedwell)	Low clumps with vertical flower spikes.	Spring
Monarda (Bee Balm)	Wild, frizzy blooms and minty-scented foliage.	Spring
Rudbeckia fulgida (Black-eyed Susan)	Late summer rays of yellow with dark centres.	Spring or autumn
Kniphofia (Red Hot Poker)	Bold, upright, and a touch exotic.	Spring
Helenium (Sneezeweed)	Warm colours and reliable performance.	Spring
Campanula (Bellflower)	Purple or white, excellent ground cover or upright.	Spring or autumn

Autumn/Fall Shrubs

Low-maintenance, high-impact, and compact enough for small gardens or containers.

Plant Name	Description	When to Plant
Viburnum opulus 'Roseum'	Snowball blooms in spring and fiery foliage in autumn.	Autumn to spring
Cotinus coggygria (Smoke Bush)	Plum-purple foliage and hazy flower plumes.	Autumn to spring
Euonymus alatus (Spindle Tree)	Flame-red autumn foliage; winged stems add winter intrigue.	Autumn to spring
Hydrangea quercifolia	Oak-leafed hydrangea with deep red autumn tones.	Autumn to spring
Cornus alba 'Sibirica'	Red stems shine in winter; foliage turns russet before falling.	Autumn to spring
Fothergilla major	Blue-green foliage that turns orange and scarlet.	Autumn
Hamamelis (Witch Hazel)	Twisty branches with fragrant, spidery flowers in winter.	Autumn to spring
Callicarpa (Beautyberry)	Glossy purple berries in autumn and winter.	Autumn
Mahonia 'Charity'	Spiky foliage and yellow flower spikes in late autumn.	Autumn to spring
Pyracantha (Firethorn)	Evergreen with bright berries; red, orange, or yellow.	Autumn to spring
Skimmia japonica	Glossy evergreen foliage and winter buds; good in shade.	Autumn to spring

Sarcococca confusa	Sweet-scented winter blooms and glossy leaves.	Autumn to spring
Rosa rugosa	Hips like tiny tomatoes and a wild, romantic habit.	Autumn to spring
Pieris japonica	New foliage in red, later white bell-shaped flowers in spring.	Autumn to spring
Chaenomeles (Flowering Quince)	Autumn pruning sets up winter structure and early spring flowers.	Autumn to spring

Autumn/Fall Climbers & Trailers

These are your living drapes and garlands, climbers that peak in autumn colour or flower, and trailers that soften edges and spill from containers.

Plant Name	Description	When to Plant
Clematis 'Bill MacKenzie'	Bright yellow nodding flowers in early autumn, followed by fluffy seedheads.	Autumn or spring
Clematis tangutica	Vigorous with lantern-like yellow blooms and silky seedheads; perfect for late-season drama.	Autumn or spring
Clematis 'Polish Spirit'	Rich purple flowers into October; vigorous and reliable.	Autumn or spring
Parthenocissus quinquefolia (Virginia Creeper)	Fiery crimson foliage in autumn; fast-growing and self-clinging.	Autumn or spring

Parthenocissus tricuspidata (Boston Ivy)	Glossy leaves that blaze red and burgundy in fall; a real wall-covering showstopper.	Autumn or spring
Lonicera periclymenum 'Serotina' (Late Dutch Honeysuckle)	Scented cream and pink blooms well into autumn.	Autumn or spring
Rosa 'Phyllis Bide'	Repeat-blooming climber with peach-pink flowers late into the season.	Autumn to early spring
Passiflora caerulea	Hardy passionflower that often continues blooming into early autumn.	Spring or autumn
Campsis radicans (Trumpet Vine)	Bold, trumpet-shaped orange-red blooms in late summer and early autumn.	Autumn or spring
Akebia quinata (Chocolate Vine)	Semi-evergreen with vanilla-scented blooms earlier, but attractive foliage in autumn.	Autumn or spring
Clematis 'Jackmanii Superba'	Deep purple blooms that often flower into October.	Autumn or spring
Hedera helix (English Ivy)	Evergreen, self-clinging, and classic. Adds structure and berries in autumn for birds.	Autumn to spring
Solanum jasminoides (Potato Vine)	Fast-growing; sometimes blooms into early fall in mild climates.	Spring or autumn
Clematis 'Madame Julia Correvon'	Rich red flowers on a compact vine; repeat flowers into early autumn.	Autumn or spring

Winter: The Quiet Wonder

Winter may seem like the garden's hush, the part where everything sleeps and not much happens, but that stillness carries its own kind of wonder. It's a season less about riotous colour and more about shape, shadow, and contrast. The garden pares back to its bones, and in doing so, reveals a quieter beauty: the elegance of bare branches etched against pale skies, the bold silhouette of a clipped evergreen, or the delicate way frost rims the edge of a hellebore leaf like nature's embroidery.

There's something deeply soothing about a winter garden. The stillness invites reflection, the air feels sharper, and the smallest signs of life, like the swelling bud of a camellia or the flicker of a robin, feel momentous. It's not loud, but it is alive. Subtle blooms appear like secrets: snowdrops breaking through the frozen ground, or witch hazel unfurling its spidery petals as if to say, "Yes, even now." The pace slows, but the reward is in noticing the little things. Winter reminds us to look closely.

This is the season for structure: clipped hedges, ornamental bark, dried seed heads dusted with frost. And for evergreens, those faithful anchors that keep the space feeling intentional and embraced. Add some berries, a few lights twinkling among bare stems, and your garden becomes not just a view, but a mood.

What to Expect in Winter

• **Strong shapes and silhouettes; topiary, grasses, and leafless branches all add drama**
With the colour dialled down, the garden becomes a study in line and form. Bare branches sketch against a frosty sky like ink on parchment, and even the humblest shrub gains gravitas when outlined in morning mist. Topiary balls and sculpted box provide architectural punctuation, nature's punctuation marks in a season of pauses.

• **Berries and seed heads that feed wildlife and lend subtle colour**
While flowers take a break, berries step into the spotlight. Crimson holly, fire-orange pyracantha, and dusky hawthorn beads all offer

bursts of colour and essential snacks for robins and blackbirds. Seed heads from summer's faded glory become buffet and shelter rolled into one.

• **Evergreens and textured foliage that offer structure and depth** Yews, box, hellebores, and glossy camellia leaves all step up when everyone else is napping. Their deep greens and rich textures hold the bones of the garden together, a living framework that keeps things from looking flat. In containers or borders, they're the strong, silent types that hold their ground with quiet dignity.

• **Winter blooms that surprise and delight in the coldest weeks** Just when you think it's all monochrome, along comes a snowdrop pushing bravely through the chill. Or a witch hazel twisting its way into bloom like yellow ribbon. Or a viburnum wafting soft scent into icy air. Winter flowers don't shout, they whisper. And that's what makes them magical.

• **A sense of peace and clarity; a garden in its simplest, most sculptural form** This is the exhale. A time for stillness, reflection, and watching the frost paint everything in silver filigree. Without the bustle of blooms, the garden becomes a calm, meditative space—a reminder that rest is not only necessary but beautiful in its own right.

Winter Shrubs

Compact, bold, fragrant, and resilient; these shrubs carry the garden through the coldest months with colour, scent, and structure.

Plant Name	Description	When to Plant
Sarcococca confusa	Small evergreen with sweetly scented winter blooms.	Autumn to spring
Daphne odora	Intensely fragrant pink blooms on evergreen foliage.	Autumn to spring
Viburnum x bodnantense	Bare branches adorned with blush-pink flowers through the frost.	Autumn to spring
Cornus sanguinea 'Midwinter Fire'	Foliage fades to reveal blazing orange-red stems.	Autumn to spring
Mahonia 'Winter Sun'	Holly-like leaves and bright yellow spires; scented and dramatic.	Autumn to spring
Skimmia japonica 'Rubella'	Red winter flower buds with dark evergreen foliage.	Autumn to spring
Witch Hazel (Hamamelis)	Spidery flowers that bloom on bare branches; citrus scent.	Autumn to spring
Camellia sasanqua	Autumn to winter-flowering variety with subtle fragrance.	Autumn
Erica carnea (Winter Heather)	Low-growing and smothered in bell-shaped blooms all winter.	Autumn
Ribes laurifolium	Unusual evergreen with pendant flower clusters in late winter.	Autumn

Lonicera fragrantissima	Winter honeysuckle with lemony flowers on bare stems.	Autumn to spring
Edgeworthia chrysantha	Paperbush, fragrant yellow pom-poms in late winter.	Autumn
Garrya elliptica	Cascading silver catkins in midwinter.	Autumn to spring
Ilex aquifolium (Holly)	Evergreen structure and bright red berries; iconic winter shape.	Autumn to spring
Chimonanthus praecox	Wintersweet; pale yellow blooms with a sweet, spicy scent.	Autumn

Winter Perennials

Tough, surprising, and often delightfully early to bloom; these keep the borders from feeling forgotten.

Plant Name	Description	When to Plant
Hellebores (Christmas Rose)	Nodding blooms in shades of white, pink, and plum, even in snow. Evergreen leaves.	Autumn to spring
Bergenia ('Elephant's Ears')	Glossy leaves with winter colour, and pink flower spikes in late winter/early spring.	Autumn to spring
Cyclamen coum	Compact plants with magenta or white flowers; patterned leaves add charm.	Autumn
Snowdrops (Galanthus)	Delicate white flowers that nod cheerfully in the coldest days.	Autumn (bulbs)

Iris unguicularis	Violet-blue flowers appear between the leaves in winter. A surprise gem.	Autumn to spring
Ajuga reptans (Bugleweed)	Evergreen ground cover with deep bronze or purple winter foliage.	Spring or autumn
Pulmonaria	Spotted leaves hold through winter; some varieties bloom in late winter.	Autumn or spring
Heuchera	Evergreen mounds in caramel, plum, and lime tones even through frost.	Spring or autumn
Eranthis hyemalis (Winter Aconite)	Buttercup-yellow blooms with delicate foliage. Cheerful and early.	Autumn (bulbs)
Arum italicum 'Marmoratum'	Marbled foliage appears in autumn and holds through winter, great for shade.	Autumn
Tiarella cordifolia	Pretty ground cover with frothy leaves and good winter persistence.	Spring or autumn
Liriope muscari (Lilyturf)	Spiky evergreen foliage with purple autumn flowers, holding form in winter.	Autumn
Carex 'Evergold'	Ornamental grass with variegated leaves; hardy and tidy in containers.	Autumn or spring

| Ophiopogon planiscapus 'Nigrescens' | Black mondo grass; dramatic, evergreen, and excellent in small spaces. | Spring or autumn |
| Helleborus foetidus ('Stinking Hellebore') | Unusual, chartreuse flowers with dark foliage; striking and long-blooming. | Autumn to spring |

Winter Climbers & Trailers

These plants provide trailing or climbing interest during winter, either through foliage, berries, or structural form.

Plant Name	Description	When to Plant
Clematis cirrhosa 'Freckles'	Evergreen with creamy bell-shaped flowers speckled with maroon in mid-winter.	Autumn or spring
Clematis armandii	Glossy evergreen leaves and scented white flowers in late winter/early spring.	Spring or autumn
Jasminum nudiflorum (Winter Jasmine)	Bare stems burst with bright yellow flowers before leaves emerge.	Autumn to spring
Hedera helix (English Ivy)	Evergreen climber with winter interest; variegated types offer brightness.	Autumn to spring
Lonicera fragrantissima (Winter Honeysuckle)	Shrubby honeysuckle with intensely fragrant blooms in late winter.	Autumn

Parthenocissus henryana	Deciduous with beautiful scarlet autumn foliage, vines add bare-branch structure in winter.	Autumn
Trachelospermum jasminoides	Evergreen jasmine that holds leaves and offers subtle winter colour; blooms in summer.	Spring or autumn
Rosa 'Madame Alfred Carrière'	Repeat-flowering climbing rose often blooms right into early winter.	Autumn to spring
Schizophragma integrifolium	Like a hydrangea vine, it offers structure in winter and blooms in summer.	Autumn
Clematis napaulensis	Winter bloomer with pale, bell-shaped flowers and fern-like foliage (it goes dormant in summer).	Spring or autumn
Actinidia kolomikta	Grows slowly but offers variegated leaves and structure; bare in winter but handsome.	Spring or autumn

Final Thoughts

A garden that thrives all year isn't built overnight. But with thoughtful planning and the right mix of plants, you'll soon find yourself enjoying something magical every month. Plant with the seasons, and you'll always have something to look forward to and talk about with anyone who dares to say gardening is "just a summer thing."

Next up: the real joy, bringing it all together. Let's keep planting, keep experimenting, and keep our wellies ready. Because every season is gardening season if you do it right.

Still Here? You Absolute Gem.

(A Note from the Author, Midway Through Your Gardening Journey)

Look at you, halfway through! That's commitment. That's compost-under-the-nails, plant-loving, tiny-space-conquering brilliance. I'm chuffed to bits you've stuck with it.

If you've had a chuckle, learned a thing or two, or felt slightly more inclined to talk sweetly to your begonias; I'd be ever so grateful if you'd consider leaving a review once you finish.

It doesn't have to be War and Peace. Just a sentence. A star or five. A kind word that helps other garden-dreamers find their way to this book.

Even better, tell a friend, post a photo of your first sprouting seedling, or show off that trellis with pride. Word of mouth grows just as beautifully as nasturtiums in a sunny spot.

Leaving a review is quick, free, and makes a big impact.

To help, simply scan the QR code and share your thoughts or click the link: [Amazon Review]

Now, on with the trowel and into the next chapter we go!
You're blooming marvellous.

Now, on with the trowel and into the next chapter we go!
You're blooming marvellous.

CHAPTER SEVEN

GREENING

Sustainable choices that save the planet

(and your pennies)

Sustainability, the gardening buzzword that's as important as compost and as trendy as houseplants on Instagram. But beyond the hashtags, embracing eco-friendly practices isn't just good for the planet, it's good for your garden, your budget, and your conscience. And the best part? You don't need to live off-grid or hug every tree (unless you really want to) to make a meaningful difference.

This chapter is your guide to greening your green space. From upcycling rubbish/trash with flair to saving every glorious drop of rainwater, we'll explore practical, planet-loving ways to make your garden a low-impact, high-joy sanctuary.

Upcycling: From Junk to Joy

Before you toss something into the bin, ask yourself: "Could I plant something in this?" If the answer is even remotely close to "probably," then congratulations, you're now an upcycler.

Tin Cans

Those empty soup tins? Clean 'em up, drill a hole in the bottom, and suddenly you've got rustic charm on a budget. Ideal for windowsills or vertical wall gardens Add a lick of paint for bonus aesthetic points

Tyres

Yes, tyres. They make bold raised beds or fun stacked planters. Stack two or three, fill with compost, and plant up a storm Paint them to avoid that "abandoned garage" vibe

Wooden Pallets

These are the Swiss Army knives of the garden world. Stand one upright for an instant vertical garden Lay one flat, line the compartments, and boom, modular raised bed

Bonus Upcycle Ideas

Broken crockery: Drainage shards for pots or mosaic decoration

Old wellies: Plant holders with character

Teapots, colanders, drawers: Quirky charm galore

Rusty ladders: Tiered plant stands with attitude

If it holds soil and makes you smile, it has a place in your sanctuary.

Water Conservation: Because Every Drop Deserves a Purpose

You don't need to live in a drought-prone area to care about water. These habits are practical, money-saving, and planet-friendly.

Daily Habits That Save Water

Water early in the morning or late in the evening to reduce evaporation..
Mulch your beds, seriously, mulch fixes nearly everything.

Cluster thirsty plants together for targeted watering.

Use a watering can for precision; it's basically yoga with water.

Accept a Little Imperfection

Don't panic over a few dry leaves, plants are tough cookies. Most won't keel over if you miss a day. They've been around longer than your hosepipe.

Rainwater Harvesting: Free Liquid Gold

Why let that glorious British downpour, or that epic American thunderstorm, go to waste when you can collect it and turn it into a free hydration station for your garden? Rainwater is softer, gentler, and much more pleasing to plants than tap water. Plus, there's something smugly satisfying about using rain to keep your cosmos perky while your neighbour wrestles with a hosepipe ban.

Whether your garden is the size of a handkerchief or you've got an entire balcony jungle, harvesting rainwater is a no-brainer.

Water Butts / Rain Barrels

• **Hook one up to your downpipe** – It's like plugging a mug into a waterfall. Once it rains (and let's be honest, it will), your butt or barrel fills up fast. Use a diverter kit to siphon off just what you need without flooding your patio. It's plumbing for beginners with a watering reward.

• **Use the water for pots, beds, or ponds** – Plants love it. No chlorine, no chemical additives, just soft, lovely H_2O. Perfect for thirsty containers, fussy foliage, and topping up wildlife ponds without distressing the tadpoles.

• **Add a filter or lid** – A lid keeps out unwanted guests: leaves, debris, and frogs who think you've installed a spa just for them. Some lids even double as planters, functional *and* fabulous. Filters help stop gunk clogging the works, especially useful in tiny gardens where smells and mess can't be hidden around the corner.

Tiny Garden Tips:

• **Choose a size that fits your space** – Mini barrels or slimline butts are ideal for patios, balconies, or side alleys. There are some truly handsome designs now that don't scream "wheelie bin" in disguise. If you're tight on room, tuck one behind a storage box or under a hanging shelf.

• **In colder regions, prep for winter** – If you're in a place that gets frosty (looking at you, North Yorkshire and Wisconsin), drain your butt before the big freeze to stop cracks. Or wrap it in old fleece or bubble wrap if you want to keep it active, just like giving your barrel a winter coat.

Smart Watering Systems: Lazy Genius Approved

Whether you've got a pocket-sized patio or a container-packed courtyard, watering smartly can save time, effort, and your plants from dramatic thirst fits. You don't need a landscaper or a spreadsheet, just a few clever tweaks that make watering feel more like a breeze and less like a guilt-ridden chore.

Drip Irrigation Ideal for the laid-back, tea-sipping gardener who likes things to just… work. Drip irrigation involves a network of thin tubes (about the width of a drinking straw) that snake around your pots or beds, with little drippers that release water *slowly* and *right* where it's needed: the roots. That means no evaporation, no soggy leaves, no wasting water.

You can run a system from a simple water butt or tap using gravity or a tiny low-voltage pump, no need to plumb in anything scary. There are full kits available online or at garden centres, many designed for DIY darlings with zero technical know-how.

Best bit? You can attach a budget-friendly timer and pretend you've hired a very obedient garden elf. Great for borders, balcony rail planters, or tightly packed container clusters where watering can access is tricky.

Soaker Hoses

Picture a hosepipe with thousands of tiny pores, basically, a garden sponge on a mission. Lay one through your beds or around large planters, turn on the tap gently, and it will seep water into the soil slowly and evenly. Very little runoff, no puddles, and the roots stay cool and hydrated, even in hot weather.

These are especially handy in slim garden strips or narrow beds along fences. You can hide them under mulch if you like to keep things looking tidy. Budget versions are widely available, and setup is as easy as connecting a hosepipe. Job done.

Self-Watering Containers

These are the unsung heroes of the forgetful, the busy, and the easily distracted. Self-watering pots usually have a hidden reservoir at the base and either a wicking system or a false bottom. Your plant draws up water as and when it fancies, no more soggy roots or bone-dry pots.

You can buy them pre-made in all sizes, from windowsill pots to large patio tubs. Or go full genius mode and make your own using a regular pot, a smaller pot or bottle inside, and a strip of cotton rope as a wick. Plants take what they need, and you get to sleep in without panic-watering your begonias.

Perfect for balconies, tiny terraces, or rented spots where low-maintenance magic is the goal.

Containers with a Conscience

Yes, your planters can be both fabulous and environmentally friendly.

Top Sustainable Choices:

Terracotta: Breathable, traditional, and recyclable (but protect from frost)

Bamboo pots: Compostable and surprisingly sturdy

Recycled plastic: Tough, lightweight, and guilt-free

Metal: Upcycled buckets, colanders, or sinks, great drainage and attitude

Avoid: Flimsy plastic that cracks in one season and ends up in landfill

Pro Tip:
Check if your local garden centre has a **pot recycling scheme**. Many do, and it's a simple way to declutter sustainably.

Wildlife-Friendly Gardening: Build It and They Will Come

A garden that's good for the planet is one that hums, chirps, rustles, and flutters. And it doesn't need to be a sprawling countryside meadow. Even the tiniest courtyard or balcony can become a sanctuary for all sorts of charming little visitors, if you offer them the right welcome mat.

The good news? Nature's not fussy. A few thoughtful tweaks and you'll have bees gossiping at your cosmos, hedgehogs snuffling through the borders, and birds forming a polite queue at your feeder.

Bug Hotels & Bee BnBs

Insect accommodation needn't be posh, but it should be varied and cosy, think rustic chic rather than five-star luxury. Use an old wooden crate or a terracotta pot on its side and fill it with rolled-up cardboard, hollow plant stems, pinecones, bark, or straw. The more crevices, the better. Ladybirds/ladybugs, solitary bees, lacewings, and all manner of pollinator pals will thank you.

Pop it in a sunny, sheltered spot, south-facing if you can, and raise it off the ground slightly to avoid soggy bottoms. You've just opened the most exclusive insect Airbnb in town.

Hedgehog Highways

Hedgehogs are garden gold, they munch on slugs, snuffle through leaves, and are frankly too cute for words. If you've got fences, cut a small hole (about 13cm x 13cm) at the base to create a hedgehog 'superhighway' between gardens. It allows them to roam freely in search of food and love (because even hedgehogs have dating lives).

And please, ditch the slug pellets. Hedgehogs eat slugs naturally, and without needing a hazmat suit afterwards.

Pollinator Buffets

Bees, butterflies, and hoverflies are essential guests in any garden. The secret to keeping them coming back? Serve up a nectar buffet from spring through autumn. Think echinacea, verbena bonariensis, salvia, and good old lavender. Choose single, open-faced flowers that let them get to the good stuff.

Avoid double-flowered varieties. They may look like floral meringues but are about as nutritious as one, too. Think "open salad bar" over "sealed cake dome."

Ponds for Everyone

You don't need a grand wildlife pond to make a splash. Even a humble washing-up bowl, an old sink, or a large plant pot saucer sunk into the soil can become an aquatic oasis. Fill it with rainwater, drop in a few pebbles, and add native plants like water forget-me-not or marsh marigold.

Crucially, provide a gentle ramp, a flat stone or piece of wood, for frogs, bees, or beetles to escape easily. No one wants a "pond of no return."

Bird Buffets

Birds are like dinner guests: if you feed them well and give them a drink, they'll keep turning up (and sometimes bring friends). Hang feeders where they feel safe, ideally near some sheltering shrubs, and keep them regularly topped up with a mix of seeds, suet, and fat balls, especially in winter.

A shallow water bath, even just a terracotta saucer on a stand, will let your feathered visitors bathe and drink. Keep it clean, refill it often, and prepare to be serenaded over your morning tea.

Composting for the Confident and the Curious

Composting isn't just for people who wear sandals with socks (although if that's you, hello, fellow enthusiast). It's easy, a little bit magical, and turns your kitchen scraps into black gold. Even better, it works in the tiniest of gardens with the right setup.

Types of Compost Bins (Especially for Small Spaces)

Whether you've got a back garden the size of a duvet or a slim courtyard, there's a composting solution that fits, stylish, sneaky, and stink-free (mostly).

Compact Compost Tumblers

Think of these as the composting equivalent of a salad spinner. They're fully enclosed, neat-looking, and ideal for patios or balconies. You pop in your greens and browns, give it a spin now and then, and it takes care of the rest. No rats. No pong. Some even come in designer colours, if you're that way inclined.

Slimline Stacking Bins (HotBins or Bokashi Towers)

Perfect for urban spots, these sleek, vertical bins take up barely any footprint and break things down fast ideal if you're the impatient gardener type. Bokashi bins are great indoors too (kitchen corner, no judgment), using special bran to ferment scraps before adding to outdoor compost or burying straight in soil.

Wormeries (For the Brave and Wiggly-Hearted)

Yes, worms. In a tidy layered system. Worms munch through scraps and give you glorious 'worm tea' for your plants (don't drink it, obviously). Great for shaded corners, balconies, or hidden behind a shed. And honestly? A bit addictive.

DIY Dustbin Method

Grab an old plastic dustbin, drill a few holes in the sides and base for airflow, and boom, you've got yourself a compost bin. Cheap, cheerful, and perfectly sized for courtyards and narrow garden strips. Just lift the lid and chuck things in. It's not fancy, but it works like a charm.

Wooden Pallet Bays (for slightly bigger spots)

If you've got room for a metre-square setup, tie three or four old pallets together to make an open compost bay. Great airflow, easy to turn, and very "country cottage with a conscience." **What to Compost:**

Green (Nitrogen-rich): Veg peelings, grass clippings, coffee grounds, tea leaves, fresh plant trimmings, and yes, **banana skins**! Full of **potassium**, which boosts plant health and flower production, and **phosphorus**, which strengthens roots. They're basically the multivitamin of compost.

Brown (Carbon-rich): Fallen leaves, toilet roll tubes, cardboard, egg boxes, straw, paper towels, shredded newspaper, and even hair (yours or your dog's, let's not be squeamish).

Bonus goodness:

• **Used coffee grounds** – Adds nitrogen and helps balance out soggy veg scraps.

• **Crushed eggshells** – Add calcium and help aerate the mix (plus: slug deterrent when crushed around plants later).

• **Old herbs/spices** – If it's plant-based and past its prime, chuck it in!

What to Avoid:

No cooked food, meat, bones, dairy, or anything oily. It'll attract every neighbourhood fox, rat, and raccoon within sniffing distance. Also avoid glossy magazines, citrus peels in large quantities (they slow the worms down), and anything treated with chemicals.

Turn Your Pile Like a Pro

Every now and then (once a fortnight if you're keen, once a month if you're honest), give your compost a mix to keep it aerated. It's basically stirring a great big pot of future flower fuel. If it smells sweet and earthy, you're doing it right. If it smells like a bin behind a dodgy takeaway, add more browns and stir bravely.

Ditch the Pesticides: Go Natural, Not Nuclear

Put down the chemical spray, darling! There's a gentler way to deal with garden troublemakers. Harsh pesticides don't just zap pests; they also harm bees, butterflies, birds, and those hardworking little beetles doing night shifts on slug patrol. In a small garden, every creature counts.

Natural Deterrents That Actually Work (No Lab Coat Required):

Garlic spray – A homemade brew (garlic cloves, water, a splash of eco-friendly soap) sends aphids packing. They hate the pong.

Neem oil – Derived from the neem tree, this miracle oil messes with pests' appetites and life cycles without harming your plants.

Soapy water – Just a few drops of washing-up liquid in a spray bottle. Brilliant for greenfly and scale insects.

Beer traps – For slugs. Sink a small cup of beer into the soil, and it turns out slugs love a pint, but sadly not the consequences.

Copper tape – Wrap it around pots to stop slugs climbing up like slimy ninjas.

Crushed eggshells or grit – Scatter around vulnerable plants to create a scratchy no-go zone for snails.

If you're dealing with persistent problems, **biological controls** like nematodes (tiny beneficial worms) can be ordered by post and watered into your soil. They target specific pests but leave everything else blissfully alone.

Plant Natives: Low-Maintenance, High-Reward

Native plants are like the locals at your garden party; they know the climate, understand the soil, and get along brilliantly with the wildlife. They tend to need less fuss, less watering, and are far more resilient in unpredictable weather.

UK Examples:

Foxglove (Digitalis purpurea) – Majestic, bee-magnet, and comes back every year if it's happy.

Primrose (Primula vulgaris) – A cheerful spring classic.

Dog Rose (Rosa canina) – A wild rose with hips for birds and bees galore.

Cow Parsley (Anthriscus sylvestris) – Softens a border like a whisper.

Yarrow (Achillea millefolium) – Flat-topped blooms in summer, great for pollinators.

US Examples (especially adaptable ones):

Purple Coneflower (Echinacea purpurea) – Drought-tolerant and glorious.

Black-eyed Susan (Rudbeckia hirta) – Sunshine on a stalk.

Milkweed (Asclepias spp.) – Essential for monarch butterflies.

Goldenrod (Solidago) – Late-summer colour and pollinator buffet.

Bee Balm (Monarda) – Scented leaves, vibrant blooms, and hummingbird heaven.

Even in a small garden, just a few native stars will invite wildlife in and make your life easier. Less pampering, more flourishing.

Final Thoughts

Sustainable gardening isn't about perfection. It's about small, intentional choices that add up. You don't need to compost like a druid or build a bug hotel worthy of five stars. Just do what you can, where you can. Every reused pot, every saved litre of water, every bird welcomed in is a tiny act of kindness; for the planet, your garden, and yourself.

Your sanctuary doesn't just have to be beautiful; it can be smart, kind, and a quietly joyful rebellion against waste.

Now then, shall we dig into the joys of year-round garden care in Chapter 8? Your plants await their seasonal spa treatment.

CHAPTER EIGHT

CARE

Seasonal maintenance that won't have you
weeping into your wheelbarrow

This chapter is your **seasonal rhythm guide**: a plant-care playlist for springtime surges, summer showstoppers, autumn wind-downs, and winter reflections. It's not about militant schedules or calendar alarms. It's about learning your garden's natural beats and doing just enough to keep things healthy, happy, and frankly, smug-looking.

But before you prune, chop, deadhead or declutter, take a moment to check your plant's preferences. Some like a spring haircut, others prefer a late-summer tidy, and a few will sulk if you even look at them the wrong way in winter. A quick online peek or a label check can save a season of regret (and confused-looking shrubs).

Spring: The Big Wake-Up

After months of doing very little but side-eyeing your sleeping garden, spring is when everything suddenly decides to burst into life, including weeds, pests, and your to-do list.

Tasks to Tackle:

Prune back dead or damaged growth on perennials, roses, and shrubs

Apply a balanced fertiliser to encourage lush, healthy growth

Begin weeding before they get smug and settle in

Refresh mulch to retain moisture and suppress weeds

Divide clumps of overcrowded perennials for free new plants

Keep an Eye On:

Slugs and snails: They're back and ravenous

Frosty surprises: Keep a fleece or cloche handy

Sudden growth spurts: Tie in climbers before they take over the patio

Pro Tip:
Spring is a great time to clean containers, oil wooden planters, and re-pot anything looking root-bound.

Summer: The Garden's Big Performance

This is peak showtime. The garden is blooming, the bees are giddy, and everything looks fabulous (or nearly). Summer maintenance is about keeping the drama going while avoiding burnout, for both you and the plants.

Tasks to Tackle:

Water deeply but less frequently to encourage strong roots

Deadhead regularly to promote new blooms and discourage seed-setting

Feed heavy bloomers and container plants every couple of weeks

Stake tall plants and climbers before they flop into your tea

Continue light weeding and check for crowding

Keep an Eye On:

Aphids, mildew, and rust; summer's not all sunshine and daisies

Wilting or yellowing leaves (could be too much or too little water)

Flowering gaps; plan autumn additions now while ideas are fresh

Pro Tip:

Water early in the morning or later in the evening, when the sun is lower and the garden feels calmer. This isn't just about efficiency, it's practically mindfulness. The air is cooler, the bees are bumbling politely, and your plants are just waking up or winding down. It's peaceful, it's grounding, and it's oddly satisfying.

Avoid watering in full midday sun; it may feel dramatic, but it's genuinely bad form. When droplets sit on leaves or petals under direct sunlight, they can act like tiny magnifying glasses, scorching the plant tissue underneath. Petals are particularly prone to turning crispy around the edges, and no one wants to look sunburned in their own flowerbed. Plus, most of the water will evaporate before it reaches the roots, which is where it's actually needed.

Think of it as the plant equivalent of avoiding a hairdryer in a heatwave. Timing matters

Autumn: The Gentle Wind-Down

Autumn isn't a sad goodbye; it's a tidy, glowing, leaf-strewn finale. This season is for clearing, planting ahead, and letting go (of your withered cosmos and overambitious cucumber dreams).

Tasks to Tackle:

Cut back spent perennials unless they offer winter interest

Plant spring bulbs, your future self will thank you

Rake up fallen leaves (make leaf mould or compost them)

Lift tender plants like dahlias and cannas for storage

Final mow and feed for lawns before it's winter nap

Keep an Eye On:

Rot and soggy patches, check drainage and clear blocked paths

Wildlife spots, leave seed heads and shelter for overwintering creatures

Pro Tip:
Autumn/Fall is the best time to assess your layout: What worked? What needs moving? Make notes now so spring-you doesn't forget.

Winter: The Quiet Reflection

Winter is not a dead zone, it's a still, structural moment. Your garden's bones are on display. Appreciate them. Do a little light care, and let the rest rest.

Tasks to Tackle:

Prune dormant trees and shrubs (especially apples and pears)

Protect vulnerable plants with fleece or straw

Clean and sharpen tools (therapeutic and weirdly satisfying)

Plan next year's layout; sketch, dream, Pinterest to your heart's content

Top up feeders and keep water out for the birds

Keep an Eye On:

Heavy snow on shrubs, gently brush it off to prevent damage

Frost pockets, raise containers off the ground

Winter interest: evergreens, bark, berries, and structure still shine

Pro Tip:

Create a cosy indoor plant corner or start planning your spring seed list by the fire. Gardening never truly stops, it just changes rhythm.

Monthly Maintenance Checklist

A month-by-month rhythm to help you stay gently in tune with your garden, not overwhelmed by it. There's no pressure to tick every box, just a little nudge in the right direction. Think of this as your seasonal companion; muddy-kneed, tea in hand, and cheering you on all the way.

January: Plan, Protect, and Ponder

Browse seed catalogues or websites – It's garden window shopping. Dream boldly, even if your space is tiny.

Check for storm damage – Loose trellis? Flapping fence panel? Better to fix it now than in gale-force conditions.

Clean pots and tools – Not thrilling, but very satisfying. Sparkling secateurs = fewer plant diseases.

Protect plants from frost – Wrap tender ones in fleece or bubble wrap. Even hardy containers appreciate a scarf.

Feed the birds – Fat balls, seeds, and fresh water help feathered friends (and natural pest control) survive the lean months.

February: Early Starts and Subtle Signs

Sow early seeds indoors – Start chill-friendly varieties on windowsills or under grow lights if you're keen.

Cut back ornamental grasses – Before new growth gets going. A quick haircut keeps things tidy and fresh.

Look for snowdrops and hellebores – Not a job, just a joy. They're the subtle drumroll of spring.

Turn compost – Give the heap a stir if it's not frozen solid. Helps wake it up for the season ahead.

Inspect overwintered plants – Check for rot, mould, or sneaky pests in your sheltered spots.

March: The Wake-Up Call

Prep your planting beds – Clear debris, weed, and add compost to feed the soil. It's like fluffing the duvet before guests arrive.

Mulch where needed – A generous layer keeps weeds down and moisture in as the weather warms.

Check containers for survivors – Some may need a top-up or a kind word. Or possibly both.

Start gentle pruning – Time to shape woody plants and remove dead stems, but only if your plant's ready for it!

Begin feeding spring bulbs – They're doing a lot of invisible work underground right now.

April: Momentum Month

Plant hardy annuals outdoors – Especially if the risk of frost is low. Check the forecast, cross fingers.

Watch for slugs and snails – Tender new growth is gourmet cuisine to them.

Mulch borders – It still counts as gardening even if you're mostly standing around with a bucket.

Tidy up paths and patios – Algae and moss can get slippery. Scrub, sweep, and claim back your stepping stones.

Keep fleece handy – Late frosts like to ruin your plans just when things start looking lovely.

May: Showtime

Harden off seedlings – Toughen them up by gradually introducing them to outdoor life. No boot camps, just fresh air.

Tie in climbers – They shoot up overnight, like teenagers. Keep them supported and politely directed.

Deadhead early bloomers – It tidies the space and encourages round two.

Pot up containers – Time to go wild with colour combos. Let your inner florist shine.

Check watering needs – Things dry out quicker now, especially in small pots and wall planters.

June: Lush and Lively

Water deeply, not daily – Roots grow stronger when they dig deep for water. Especially important in containers.

Stake or support tall plants – Wind, rain, or sheer enthusiasm can send them flopping otherwise.

Prune spring shrubs post-flower – Keeps them neat and encourages better blooms next year.

Weed little and often – Do a lap with a hand fork and you'll stay ahead of the jungle.

Feed flowering plants – Think of it as buying them a drink after all their hard work.

July: Full Bloom Energy

Deadhead regularly – Like clearing confetti after a party, keeps things fresh and blooming.

Weed, again (and again) – The more you do now, the less you'll curse in August.

Water containers thoroughly – In the morning or evening, not at lunchtime sunbathing hours.

Watch for mildew or aphids – Warm, muggy days are a pest paradise. Spot early, act gently.

Keep feeding – Hanging baskets and planters are hungry little things.**August: High Summer HustleHarvest joyfully** – Flowers, seeds, foliage; whatever's thriving, snip it and enjoy it indoors or in a posy.

Cut hedges now – Before birds start nesting again or shrubs get too shaggy.

Keep up with watering – Group pots together for easier reach and shared humidity.

Take cuttings – A thrifty way to make new plants from old favourites.

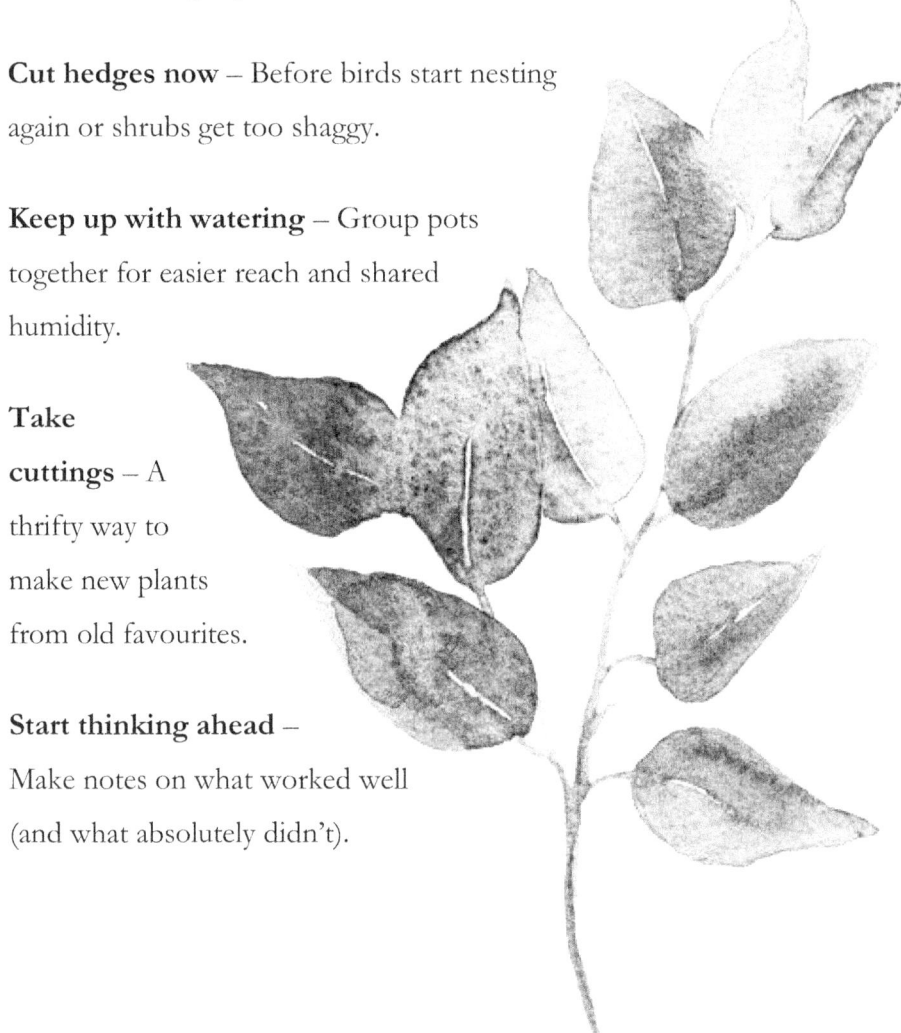

Start thinking ahead – Make notes on what worked well (and what absolutely didn't).

September: Shift the Tempo

Divide overgrown perennials – Share them with friends or fill new gaps.

Plant spring bulbs – Daffodils, crocus, and snowdrops go in now for future joy.

Collect and label seeds – Use paper envelopes, not mystery drawers of doom.

Tidy and mulch borders – Keeps things smart and helps with winter prep.

Keep deadheading – Some late bloomers just need encouragement.

October: The Gentle Wrap-Up

Clear out summer annuals – Compost the ones that are fading gracefully.

Lift tender plants – Dahlias and cannas might need to come in for winter holidays.

Sweep up leaves – Make leaf mould or compost, gold dust for next year.

Clean and store garden furniture – Unless you're very committed to outdoor tea in November.

Cut back faded perennials – Or leave them for winter structure and wildlife.

November: Tuck It All In

Plant bare-root roses and shrubs – Great time to get roots established before spring.

Wrap pots – Use fleece or bubble wrap to protect from cracking.

Empty rain butts slightly – Make room for winter rain and avoid overflow.

Rake paths and patios – Wet leaves are like banana skins in disguise.

Keep feeding birds – They're working harder than ever to find snacks now.

December: Peaceful Pause

Admire the structure – Bare stems, seed heads, frosted branches; your garden's bones are beautiful.

Plan next year's layout – Sketch ideas, update your wish list, maybe browse for fancy secateurs.

Clean tools and sort shed corners – The kind of job you'll thank yourself for in spring.

Decorate with natural cuttings – Holly, ivy, rosemary; all fair game for festive flair.

Put your feet up – You've earned it. The garden is resting, and so should you.

Final Thoughts

Seasonal plant maintenance isn't about perfection, it's about rhythm. A gentle, sometimes mucky dance between you and your garden, responding to the cues of nature. Get into the habit of seasonal check-ins, and your sanctuary will reward you with resilience, beauty, and endless moments of joy.

Now, pop the kettle on.

Next up: pests, diseases, and what to do when something small decides to munch your masterpiece.

CHAPTER NINE

TROUBLE

Pests, problems, and other leafy dramas

Let's face it, pests and plant diseases are the uninvited guests at your garden party. Just when your roses are looking ravishing or your geraniums are in full smug bloom, something sneaky, six-legged, or spotty decides to move in. But before you panic-Google "DIY flamethrower," let's take a deep breath.

This chapter is all about staying one step ahead, working with nature, and keeping your sanctuary thriving without turning your garden into a chemical battlefield. With a little know-how, a few eco-friendly tricks, and some helpful garden allies, you'll soon be pest-prepared and fungus-fortified.

Prevention First: Garden Vigilante Mode

The best way to stop pests and diseases is to catch them before they throw a party.

Daily Walkabouts (Cup of Tea Optional)

Stroll through your garden like a plant detective.

Look under leaves, along stems, and around new growth.

Holes? Spots? Fuzzy patches? That's your cue.

Strong Soil, Strong Plants

Feed your soil with compost and mulch, it builds plant resilience.

Healthy soil = happy roots = tougher plants.

Rotate crops if growing edibles to avoid soil-borne nasties.

Space and Airflow

Crowded plants = fungal fiesta.

Give plants room to breathe. Especially in containers or shady corners.

Clean Tools = Clean Plants

Wipe your tools after use (especially between pruning jobs).

Dirty trowels spread more gossip and diseases than a chatty robin.

Meet Your Pest Patrol: Garden Heroes

Why battle bugs when you can recruit natural assassins?

Ladybirds (Ladybugs in the US) Aphid eaters extraordinaire. Attract with dill, fennel, marigolds, and cosmos.

Hoverflies Their larvae devour aphids and whitefly. Grow yarrow, alyssum, and parsley to invite them in.

Frogs and Toads Eat slugs like they're tapas. A small pond or damp log pile makes them feel right at home.

Birds Wrens, robins, and finches love caterpillars. Offer feeders in winter and a birdbath year-round.

Hedgehogs (UK-specific, but adorable worldwide) Munch slugs and beetles all night long. Make small holes in fences for access and ditch toxic slug pellets.

Pests, Plagues & Cheeky Culprits

Let's name and shame the usual suspects and how to handle them.

Aphids (Greenfly, Blackfly)

Clusters on new shoots. Leaves curl and yellow.

Solution: Spray with diluted soapy water, blast with a hose, or recruit ladybirds/ladybugs.

Slugs and Snails

Tell-tale slime trails and chewed leaves. Especially fond of hostas and seedlings.

Solution: Copper tape, beer traps, crushed eggshells, or night patrol with a torch

Powdery Mildew

White, powdery coating on leaves.

Thrives in dry soil with humid air.

Solution: Improve airflow, water at roots, prune affected parts

Rust & Leaf Spot

Orange or black blotches on leaves. Often appears in wet

conditions.

Solution: Remove affected leaves, space plants, and compost mindfully (not diseased leaves).

Vine Weevil

Leaves notched; roots eaten by grubs. Affects container plants

Solution: Pick off adults at night, use nematodes or sticky traps

Caterpillars

Holes in leaves, sometimes entire plants devoured. Look under leaves for eggs or larvae

Solution: Hand-pick or cover plants with mesh netting

Natural Deterrents: Gentle But Firm

Put the chemicals down, these clever methods are safer, cheaper, and far more satisfying.

Soapy Water Spray

A few drops of dish soap in a litre of water. Spray aphid-infested leaves (underside too!)

Garlic & Chilli Spray

Blend garlic, chilli, and water; strain and spray. Smells like trouble (to pests, not vampires).

Neem Oil

Organic and highly effective on many insects. Disrupts pest life cycles without harming beneficial bugs.

Companion Planting

Nasturtiums: Lure aphids away from your prized plants
Marigolds: Repel nematodes and other soil-born baddies
Basil near tomatoes: Deters whitefly and adds aroma

Diatomaceous Earth

A fine powder from fossilised algae. Cuts through soft-bodied insects (safe for pets, not for bugs)

DIY Barriers & Blocks

Sometimes, a good fence (or net) makes great neighbours.

Copper Tape: Repels slugs from pots

Fine Mesh Netting: Keeps butterflies off brassicas (sorry, cabbage whites)

Slug Collars: Circular shields for vulnerable seedlings

Cloche Covers: Protect new plants from pests, frost, and overly curious pigeons

When Things Go Wrong: Plant First Aid

Even the best gardens have off days. Plants are living things, after all, not plug-and-play garden ornaments. But with a bit of observation and a lot of curiosity, most hiccups can be solved without needing a degree in botany or a stiff gin.

Here's your cheat sheet for diagnosing the greenroom drama and getting things back on track:

Leaves Turning Yellow?

What it might be: Overwatering, underwatering, poor drainage, or a nutrient imbalance. Sometimes it's just stress. We've all been there.

What to try: Stick your finger in the soil. Dry? Water it. Wet and soggy? Improve drainage. Use a balanced liquid feed to perk up tired roots. If older leaves are yellowing but new ones are fine, don't panic, it might just be natural ageing.

Droopy Plants?

What it might be: Bone-dry roots or root rot from soggy soil. Either way, your plant is in crisis talks.

What to try: Gently remove the plant from its pot and check the roots. Mushy and brown = rot. Bone dry and brittle = thirst.. Repot with fresh compost if things look dire, and adjust your watering routine to avoid future drama.

Brown Tips on Leaves?

What it might be: Low humidity, inconsistent watering, overfeeding, or salt build-up from fertiliser. Think crispy salad edges.

What to try: Mist the leaves in the morning (unless it's fuzzy foliage). Flush the soil with clean water once a month to wash away salts. Ease up on the fertiliser, less is often more.

No Flowers?

What it might be: Too much nitrogen (hello, leaf jungle), not enough sun, or pruning at the wrong time.
What to try: Switch to a bloom-boosting fertiliser with higher potassium. Move the plant to a sunnier spot if it's sulking in shade. Google your plant's pruning calendar—some only flower on last year's growth, and you might've snipped their dreams.

Chewed, Mottled, or Spotted Leaves?

What it might be: Pests. Possibly aphids, caterpillars, spider mites, or something with far too many legs.
What to try: Inspect the undersides of leaves. Use a magnifying glass if you're feeling Sherlock-y. Try a gentle soap spray or neem oil. For slugs and snails, try crushed eggshells, beer traps, or lure them elsewhere with sacrificial lettuce.

Leaves Falling Off Prematurely?

What it might be: Sudden temperature shifts, overwatering, or sheer indignation. Some houseplants are drama queens.
What to try: Check for drafts or heat sources. Let the soil dry

slightly between watering. Reassure the plant, sometimes they just need time to adjust to new surroundings.

Wilting Despite Watering?

What it might be: Heat stress, poor root development, or compacted soil that water can't penetrate.
What to try: Shade the plant during the hottest part of the day.. Loosen the soil gently with a fork.. Add mulch to keep the roots cool and moist.

Spots on Leaves?

What it might be: Fungal disease, bacterial leaf spot, or mildew. It's less glamorous than it sounds.
What to try: Remove affected leaves with clean scissors.. Improve air circulation, crowded plants = fungus party.. Use an organic fungicide or make your own with baking soda and water.

The Drama-Free Garden Mindset

Some damage is part of the deal. Holes in leaves? Nature's confetti. A few aphids? Garden protein for your ladybirds/ladybugs. As long as your plants are mostly healthy and still growing, there's no need to panic.

Final Thoughts

Keeping pests and diseases at bay doesn't require military precision or a PhD in entomology. It just takes attentiveness, a dash of patience, and a little help from your garden's natural allies. With proactive habits, eco-friendly tricks, and clever planting, your sanctuary can stay serene, safe, and gloriously full of life, minus the unwanted visitors. Resist perfection. Aim for balance.

So go on, walk your garden beat, keep those ladybirds/ladybugs well-fed, and remember: the only drama you want in your garden is from your dahlias, not your aphids.

Next up: all those handy tips, tricks, and sanity-savers that every gardener should keep in their back pocket.

CHAPTER TEN

FINISHING

Final touches to make your garden sing
(or at least politely hum)

By now, you're well on your way to becoming a bona fide garden whisperer; muddy-kneed, plant-savvy, and just a little bit smug (in the nicest possible way). This chapter is your final grab-bag of advice: the shortcuts, secrets, and sanity-saving wisdom that help you avoid common pitfalls and squeeze even more joy out of your sanctuary.

No fluff, no faff; just the clever things every gardener wishes they'd known sooner.

Shady Characters: Plants for Low-Light CornersTop Shady Picks:

Whether you're working with a north-facing nook, a patch beneath a tree, or a narrow side passage that gets more gloom than glow, shade doesn't have to mean dull. These plants **thrive in dappled or partial shade**, bring colour and texture, and help you build that cool, woodland-inspired calm.

Hostas *Perennial* • *Plant in spring or autumn* Leafy legends with dramatic foliage—from zingy lime to smoky blue. Perfect for borders, containers, or making a splash near ponds. Watch for slugs like a hawk; they think hostas are a buffet. Use grit, copper tape, or place sacrificial decoys.

Ferns *Perennial* • *Plant in spring or autumn* Bring texture and movement with classics like **Dryopteris** (male fern) or **Asplenium** (hart's tongue). Ideal for shaded containers or under trees. No flowers, but the sculptural fronds do all the talking.

Astilbes *Perennial* • *Plant in spring or autumn* Feathery, frothy plumes in white, pink, or deep red. Great in damp, shaded areas—think beside sheds or under trees where the soil stays cool. Mulch in spring to keep them happy.

Heucheras (Coral Bells) *Perennial • Plant in spring or early autumn*
Low-growing foliage stars with dramatic colours: marmalade, blood red, dusky purple. Pretty enough for pots, tough enough for borders. Tiny flowers in summer are just a bonus.

Lungwort (Pulmonaria) *Perennial ground cover • Plant in autumn or early spring*
Silver-speckled leaves and early flowers in pinks, blues, and purples. A shade garden is essential for that "woodland carpet" look. Bees adore it, and it copes well in dry shade once established.

Foxgloves (Digitalis) *Biennial or short-lived perennial • Sow seeds in summer, plant in spring*
Towering elegance with bell-shaped blooms in creamy whites, soft pinks, and purples. Dappled shade is perfect. Let them self-seed for a naturalistic display year after year.

Brunnera (False Forget-Me-Not) *Perennial • Plant in spring or autumn*
Heart-shaped, silvery leaves and dainty blue flowers in spring. Beautiful in borders or as ground cover in shadier zones. A quieter plant, but with huge impact.

Tiarella (Foam Flower) *Perennial ground cover* • *Plant in spring or autumn*
Similar to heucheras but with soft, foamy white flowers. Excellent under shrubs or in containers where sunlight is scarce. Leaves often turn bronze in autumn for added interest.

Hydrangea 'Annabelle' or 'Paniculata' *Shrub* • *Plant in spring or autumn*
Tolerant of part-shade, especially morning sun/afternoon shade. Huge, showy flowerheads add drama and a romantic touch to even the smallest urban garden.

Ivy (Hedera helix) *Evergreen climber* • *Plant anytime the ground isn't frozen*
Hardy, classic, and excellent for vertical interest in shady spots. Choose a variegated variety to brighten darker corners, but do keep it trimmed or it'll start redecorating your home too.

Hellebores (Lenten Rose) *Perennial* • *Plant in autumn or spring*
Winter-blooming and utterly charming. Flower colours range from soft white to dusky plum, blooming when everything else is snoozing. Perfect for woodland-style planting.

Tip:

Layer with foliage first, flowers second. Texture makes the shade sing.

The Art of Watering: Not Too Much, Not Too Little

Watering is part science, part instinct and part forgetting, then panicking. Let's make it easier.

Watering Wisdom:

Water early morning or late evening to reduce evaporation

Deep, less frequent watering = stronger roots

Use watering cans or drip hoses for precision

Water the soil, not the leaves, wet foliage = mildew central

Pots dry quickly, check daily in hot weather

Quick Test:

Stick your finger into the soil. If it's dry up to your second knuckle, give it a drink. If not, hands off.

Re-potting: Give Roots Room to Roam

Plants like personal space too. If they're root-bound, growth slows and watering gets wonky.

Signs It's Time:

Roots growing out of drainage holes

Water runs straight through

The plant looks stunted or top-heavy

How To Re-pot:

Choose a pot one size up

Gently loosen the roots (trim any circling ones)

Use fresh peat-free compost

Water well and let it recover in light shade

Bonus:

Divide clump-formers like hostas and ornamental grasses—free plants!

Fertilisers: Feed Me, Seymour

Plants get hangry too. Here's what to serve:

Eco-Friendly Options:

Compost: Homegrown nutrient magic

Seaweed extract: Boosts root health and resilience

Worm castings: Natural slow-release food

Comfrey tea: Stinks, but plants love it

Well-rotted manure: Ideal for borders and heavy feeders

Traditional Fertilisers:

Slow-release pellets: Easy, long-lasting

Liquid feeds: Great for containers and quick results

Specialised feeds: Tomato food, rose food, etc; tailored nutrients

Tips: Feed during active growing seasons (spring and summer). Follow the instructions, more is not better. Rotate feeds to avoid build-up of specific elements

Budget Gardening Hacks: Big Beauty, Little Cost

You don't need a big budget for big impact.

Top Frugal Fixes:

Grow from seed: Cheaper, more variety, immensely satisfying

Swap plants with friends or neighbours

Use supermarket herbs as starter plants (repot immediately!)

Reuse containers: Teapots, tins, and even old colanders

Join local gardening groups for freebies and advice

DIY Upgrades:

Paint tired pots for an instant refresh

Create plant markers from lolly sticks or wine corks

Make a trellis from old bamboo canes or branches

Finishing Touches: Charm, Quirk & A Dash of Magic

Once the plants are planted, the mulch is mulched, and the birds are singing, what next? That's when you get to have a bit of fun. These are the *personality pieces*, the final flourishes that give your garden its own voice. Think less 'posh garden parade' and more 'your backyard with a little sparkle and swagger. Here are a few of our favourite extras to turn your outdoor space from lovely to utterly irresistible:

Outdoor Mirrors

Want your tiny courtyard to feel like it leads to Narnia? Pop up a garden mirror. They bounce light into shadier corners and add a bit of Alice-in-Wonderland mystery. Just don't place them where birds might mistake them for open air and attempt high-speed introductions.

Windchimes

The soundtrack of calm. A gentle breeze and soft tinkling can make your space feel positively meditative. Just avoid anything that sounds like a haunted xylophone, especially if you have easily startled neighbours or twitchy pets.

Garden Lights

Whether it's twinkling fairy lights, solar lanterns, or a classy wall sconce, lighting extends your garden's hours of charm into the evening. Pop a string through a tree, wrap them round a trellis, or line a path with tiny glowing mushrooms. Practical? Not always. Magical? Always.

Gnomes

Love them or loathe them, gnomes are the cheeky houseguests of the garden world. Place one peering through a shrub, balancing on a wall, or emerging dramatically from a hosta. Bonus points if it makes people laugh, or mildly unsettles them.

Outdoor Clocks

Perfect for those who like to potter with purpose. A big Roman numeral clock on the wall of a shed or fence says, "Yes, I am aware it's nearly tea time." Choose one that's weatherproof and won't start losing minutes faster than a distracted gardener.

Weather Vanes

Because why *wouldn't* you want to know which way the wind's blowing in your five square metres of sanctuary? From classic roosters to flying pigs or vintage bicycles, they add a touch of quirky tradition and give you something to point at dramatically during garden chats

Beginner FAQs: Quick Answers for Common Wobbles

How often should I water? Depends on the plant, the pot, and the weather. Poke your finger into the soil—if it feels like a damp sponge, hold off. If it's dry an inch down, it's time to give it a drink. Trust your finger more than the calendar.

What's the easiest plant to start with? Lavender, nasturtiums, marigolds, and hardy geraniums are all low-drama stars. If you're feeling brave, add mint—but only in a pot, unless you fancy mint taking over your life.

Can I plant in winter? Not much in terms of seeds, but it's a great time for bare-root trees, shrubs, and roses. Plus, you can plan and prune to your heart's content. Garden dreaming is practically a winter sport.

Why did my plant suddenly die? Check the roots; too wet, too dry, or something nasty nibbling? Sometimes it's just garden roulette. It happens to the best of us. Plant something else and carry on.

How do I stop killing houseplants? Light, airflow, and a strict no-soggy-feet policy. Water only when needed, rotate occasionally, and yes talking to them does no harm. Singing optional but encouraged.

Do I need to feed my plants? Eventually, yes. Container plants especially need a bit of lunch now and then. Use a balanced feed in growing season. It's like vitamins for your begonias.

Why are my leaves turning brown/crispy? Usually underwatering, sunburn, or dry indoor air. Move them, mist them, or give them a proper soak. Occasionally, it's just a dramatic leaf shedding its mortal coil.

Can I plant directly into bags of compost? Yes! Especially for things like salads, herbs, and even potatoes. Just slice open the bag, fluff up the soil, and pop in your plants. It's scruffy brilliance.

Why are my seeds not sprouting? Old seeds? Too cold? Too wet? Too deep? Seeds can be fussy. Try again with fresh seed and a warm windowsill. Failing that, cheat with plug plants.

Do I need loads of tools? Not at all. Start with a trowel, secateurs, and a watering can. The rest can wait until the birthday list rolls around.

What's the best advice for beginners? Start small. Choose things you like. Don't worry about rules. Plants want to grow— your job is just to help them along.

Final Thoughts

Gardening is part science, part art, and part glorious, mucky improvisation. There's always something to learn, something to tweak, and something to chuckle at. The real trick is not to chase perfection, it's to enjoy the process.

So keep these tips handy. Refer back when in doubt. And always remember: if all else fails, mulch it and move on.

Next up: we wrap it all up with a final muddy flourish in the conclusion.

CHAPTER ELEVEN

FAREWELL

A cup of tea and a quiet hooray; you did it!

And just like that, we've reached the final stepping stone on this garden path. If you're still here, and I do hope you are, perhaps slightly muddy and a touch windblown, then congratulations, dear reader: you are well on your way to becoming a sanctuary gardener. Not the perfectly-pruned, Latin-spouting, white-gloved sort (unless, of course, that's your vibe, in which case, you wear those gloves with pride), but the *real* kind: thoughtful, joyful, a little cheeky, and totally in tune with your precious little patch of Earth.

You've planned, sketched, and possibly colour-coded. You've wrangled spades, embraced compost, and made peace with the idea that snails are tenacious little

147

sods. You've designed spaces, picked focal points, and fallen mildly in love with at least three plants that you swore you'd just browse and not buy.

You now understand soil like a horticultural detective, have learned that 'full sun' is not a polite suggestion, and know that vertical gardening is just showing off, but in a fabulous way. You've embraced the seasons, accepted the odd nibble from a pest, and turned setbacks into compostable lessons.

And more than anything, you've created something from nothing. Something beautiful. Something imperfectly perfect that's growing, changing, and rooting itself into your days. A sanctuary that gives as much as it takes; a space for morning tea, quiet chats, muddy knees, and perhaps one too many gnomes. (We don't judge here.)

Because this isn't just about plants, it's about peace. About play. About moments of connection with something real. It's about standing in your tiny outdoor space with your hands on your hips and thinking, *"Look what I made."* Even if what you made is mostly foliage and a suspiciously smug pigeon.

So here's to you: To the sanctuary you've grown, one pot and pruning mishap at a time. To the laughter, the learning, the failed experiments that somehow sprouted anyway. To the beauty, the stillness, the joy of a single bloom showing up right on cue.

Keep experimenting. Keep learning. Keep sipping tea while staring thoughtfully at a leaf like it's telling you its secrets. Most of all, keep enjoying every muddy, miraculous moment.

The garden is calling. Off you go.

Help Your Garden Grow… and This Book Too!

Share your thoughts, sow some kindness, and help future gardeners blossom.

"A kind word is like a spring rain." – *Proverb (probably whispered by a flower)*

You've made it through the weeds, the worms, the witty bits, and hopefully you're now staring at your very own patch of paradise, muddy boots and all. If this book made you smile, sparked a garden dream, or simply gave you the nudge to finally buy that trowel… then I have one teeny favour to ask:

Would you leave a review? Your words, yes, even just a sentence or two; could be the very thing that helps someone else decide to begin their garden journey. And not just any garden, a *sanctuary*. Your review could be the seed that grows:

- One more windowsill of cheery violas
- One more tiny courtyard filled with bees and calm
- One more afternoon of peace for someone juggling life
- One more person realising they *can* garden, even in a teacup
- One more neighbour realising the gnome is always watching

It only takes a moment, but it means the world. Your review helps this little book reach more hopeful green fingers and thumbs just like you.

If you've laughed, learned, or even just liked the line about airborne geraniums, please pop over and let me know.

Leaving a review is quick, free, and makes a big impact.

To help, simply scan the QR code and share your thoughts or click the link: [Amazon Review]

Now, on with the trowel and into the next chapter we go!
You're blooming marvellous.

 Thank you, truly, for being part of this gentle revolution; one pot, one petal, one patch at a time.

With muddy gratitude and a rusty watering can salute.

GLOSSARY

Green terms made simple (no Latin required)

Whether you're wielding a trowel in Tunbridge Wells or watering tomatoes in Toledo, this glossary bridges the Atlantic gap with cheerful clarity. Gardening doesn't need to sound like science class, these are the terms you'll see sprinkled throughout the book (and beyond), with no Latin degree required.

Term	Definition	UK/US Notes
Annual	A plant that completes its life cycle in one growing season	Same both sides
Biennial	Grows leaves in the first year, flowers the second, then dies	Same both sides
Perennial	Lives for more than two years, often blooming each season	Same both sides
Border	A bed or area where plants grow, often along an edge	Same both sides
Compost	Decomposed organic matter used to feed soil and plants	Same both sides

Peat-free compost	Compost made without peat, to protect bog ecosystems	Widely promoted in UK; gaining traction in US
Greywater / Graywater	Gently used household water (e.g. bathwater) repurposed for watering	Greywater (UK), Graywater (US)
Deadheading	Snipping off spent flowers to encourage new blooms	Same both sides
Hardy	Can survive winter outdoors	Same both sides
Tender	Needs protection from cold/frost	Same both sides
Mulch	A layer (bark, compost, straw) placed on soil to lock in moisture, suppress weeds, and improve structure	Same both sides
Pollinator	Insects (like bees and butterflies) that help plants reproduce by moving pollen	Same both sides
Container	A pot, trough, bucket or anything that holds soil and plants	Same both sides
Water butt / Rain barrel	A container that collects rainwater from a roof	Water butt (UK), Rain barrel (US)
Upcycling	Turning something old or unused into something useful in the garden (e.g. a teapot planter)	Same both sides
Propagation	Creating new plants from seeds, cuttings, or division	Same both sides
Raised bed	A garden bed built above ground level, often in a frame or box	Same both sides

No-dig	A method of gardening where soil is not turned over, preserving structure and life	Popular in both regions
Soil pH	A measure of acidity/alkalinity in soil—affects what can grow well	Same both sides
Loam	The holy grail of soil: a mix of sand, silt, and clay with great drainage and nutrients	Same both sides
Hardening off	Gradually acclimating indoor-grown plants to outdoor life	Same both sides
Cloche	A cover (plastic, glass, fabric) that protects plants from cold	Same both sides
Top dressing	A layer of compost or feed applied on the surface of soil	Same both sides
Leggy	A plant that's grown tall and spindly due to lack of light	Same both sides
Cuttings	A piece of a plant (stem, leaf, or root) used to grow a new plant	Same both sides
Green manure	A crop grown to be dug back into the soil to enrich it	Same both sides
Self-seeding	When plants drop their own seeds and grow new plants without you lifting a finger	Same both sides
Hard prune / Soft prune	Hard: heavy cutting back. Soft: gentle trim to shape or maintain	Same both sides
Wicking system	A self-watering setup using a wick to draw water from a reservoir to the soil	Common in small-space gardening

Pollard / Coppice	Traditional tree pruning methods for managing size and shape	More common in UK
Bolting	When plants (often leafy ones) flower prematurely, usually due to heat	Same both sides
Chitting	Letting seed potatoes sprout before planting (a very British pastime)	Common term in UK; lesser-known in US

REFERENCES

Because even gardeners need to cite their sources

Here are some of the resources, books, and websites that inspired or supported the information shared in this book. They're great companions for deepening your knowledge or just having a nose around on a rainy day.

Books

Beth Chatto's Gravel Garden by Beth Chatto – A classic for sustainable, dry gardening.

The Dry Garden by Beth Chatto – Perfect for those tricky, parched spots.

Down to Earth by Monty Don – A warm and insightful read from Britain's favourite muddy boots.

The Well-Tempered Garden by Christopher Lloyd – Witty, wise, and wildly useful.

Planting: A New Perspective by Piet Oudolf and Noel Kingsbury – Great for understanding planting design and naturalistic styles.

Websites

Royal Horticultural Society (RHS) – www.rhs.org.uk
Brilliant for plant profiles, growing guides, and pest advice.

Garden Organic – www.gardenorganic.org.uk
Ideal for eco-friendly gardening resources.

BBC Gardeners' World – www.gardenersworld.com
Tips, videos, and seasonal inspiration.

Organisations

The Wildlife Trusts – Great for wildlife-friendly gardening tips.

Soil Association – For guidance on organic standards and composting.

National Garden Scheme (NGS) – For garden visit inspiration and supporting community gardens.

Whether you're leafing through a book, scrolling through a guide, or having a good old chat with fellow garden lovers, knowledge is your best companion. Keep learning, keep exploring, and keep growing.

Printed in Great Britain
by Amazon